MAZES
FOR
BRIGHT
SPARKS

Puzzles and solutions by
Dr Gareth Moore
B.Sc (Hons) M.Phil Ph.D

Introducing the Maze Master:
Gareth Moore, B.Sc (Hons) M.Phil Ph.D

Dr Gareth Moore is an Ace Puzzler and author
of many puzzle and brain-training books.

He created online brain-training site, BrainedUp.com,
and runs online puzzle site, PuzzleMix.com. Gareth has
a Ph.D from the University of Cambridge, where he
taught machines to understand spoken English.

Illustrations by Jess Bradley

Designed by Zoe Bradley
and Derrian Bradder
Edited by Helen Brown
Cover design by Angie Allison

MAZES

FOR
BRIGHT SPARKS

Buster Books

First published in Great Britain in 2020 by Buster Books,
an imprint of Michael O'Mara Books Limited,
9 Lion Yard, Tremadoc Road, London SW4 7NQ

W www.mombooks.com/buster f Buster Books 🐦 @BusterBooks 📷 @buster_books

Puzzles and solutions © Gareth Moore 2020
Illustrations and layouts © Buster Books 2020

A CIP catalogue record for this book is available
from the British Library.

ISBN: 978-1-78055-661-1

2 4 6 8 10 9 7 5 3

Papers used by Buster Books are natural, recyclable products made of wood from
well-managed, FSC®-certified forests and other controlled sources. The manufacturing
processes conform to the environmental regulations of the country of origin.

Printed and bound in August 2021 by CPI Group (UK) Ltd,
108 Beddington Lane, Croydon, CR0 4YY, United Kingdom

INTRODUCTION

Mazes are puzzles that absolutely anyone can solve and they come in loads of different shapes and sizes.

The mazes in this book are made up of branching passages through which you must find a route. Some routes follow the 'In' to the 'Out' and others follow a route to the middle of the maze.

Whether the mazes are rectangular, triangular, hexagonal or circular, the walls are fixed, so you cannot jump over them. If you come to a dead end, you must turn around and try again, so use a pencil in case you make a mistake.

The mazes in this book get tougher as the book progresses. There are four difficulty levels – Rising Star, Shooting Star, Super Star and Supernova.

You can time yourself, too, if you like. There's a space at the end of each page to note your time. All the answers are at the back of the book.

Good luck, and have fun!

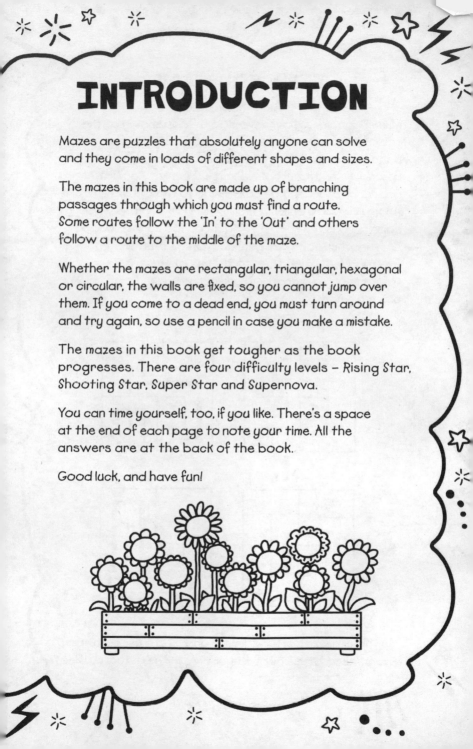

FIND YOUR WAY

Multi-floor maze

Multi-floor mazes have two floors – one shown at the top of the page and the other at the bottom of the page. Within each floor, there are numbers which act as ladders to travel between the different floors. When you reach a ladder, you can climb it to travel to the other floor – or carry on past if you wish.. For example, if you come across the number '1', look for the corresponding '1' in another floor and continue your path there. Not every ladder will lead you to the end of the maze; some will lead you to a dead end and you will have to go back and try a new route.

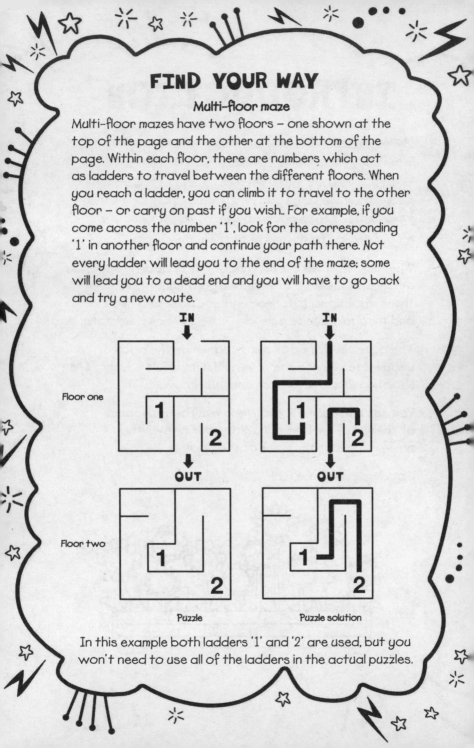

Floor one

Floor two

Puzzle   Puzzle solution

In this example both ladders '1' and '2' are used, but you won't need to use all of the ladders in the actual puzzles.

Warp maze

A warp maze works like a multi-floor maze, except that it has magic ladders that 'warp' you to another point in the same maze. When you reach a magic ladder, marked with a letter, you can continue from another copy of the same letter elsewhere in the grid – or you can pass over it and continue along the path. Just watch out for dead ends!

For example, if you reach an 'A' then you can choose to continue from another 'A' in the same grid.

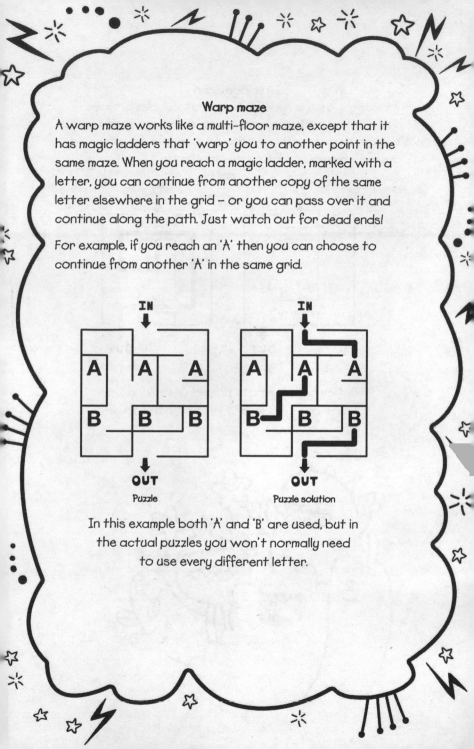

Puzzle

Puzzle solution

In this example both 'A' and 'B' are used, but in the actual puzzles you won't normally need to use every different letter.

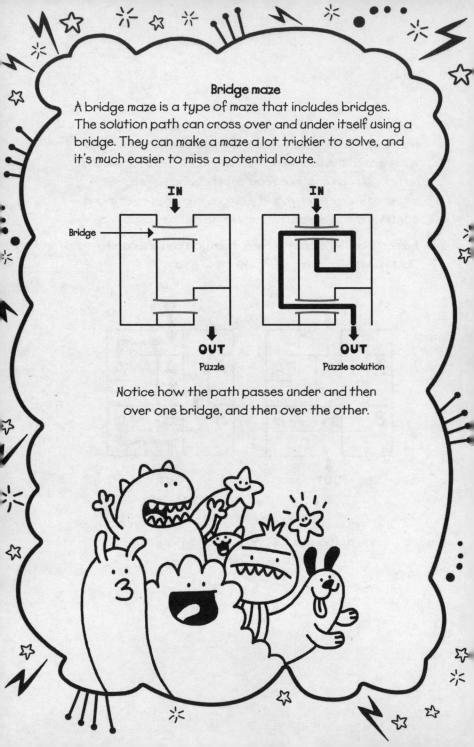

Bridge maze

A bridge maze is a type of maze that includes bridges.
The solution path can cross over and under itself using a
bridge. They can make a maze a lot trickier to solve, and
it's much easier to miss a potential route.

IN

IN

Bridge →

OUT

Puzzle

OUT

Puzzle solution

Notice how the path passes under and then
over one bridge, and then over the other.

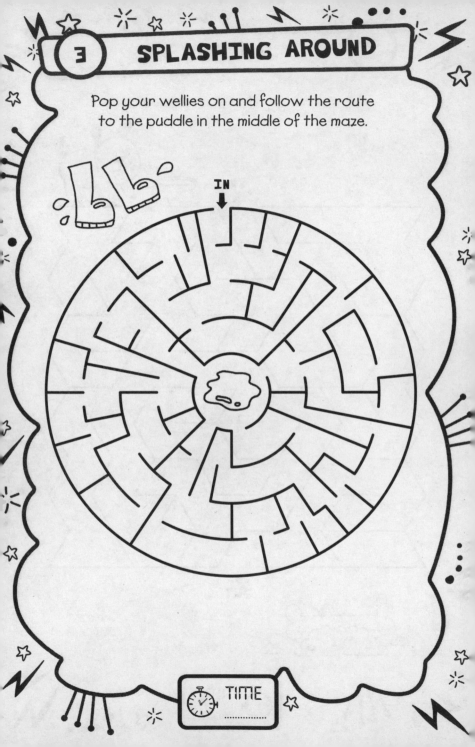

3 SPLASHING AROUND

Pop your wellies on and follow the route
to the puddle in the middle of the maze.

IN

TIME

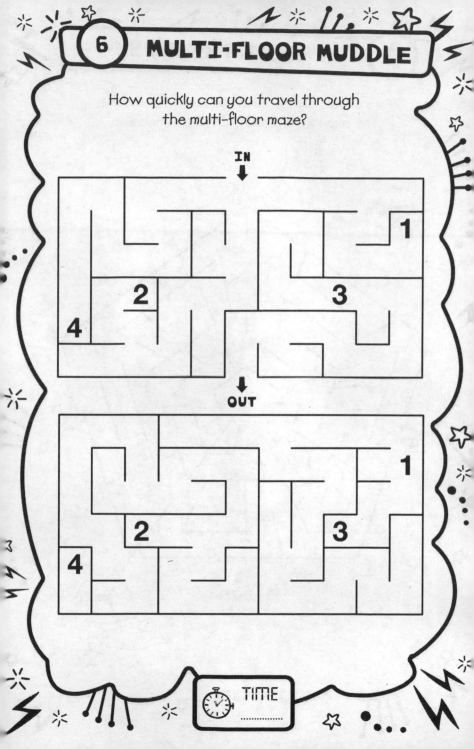

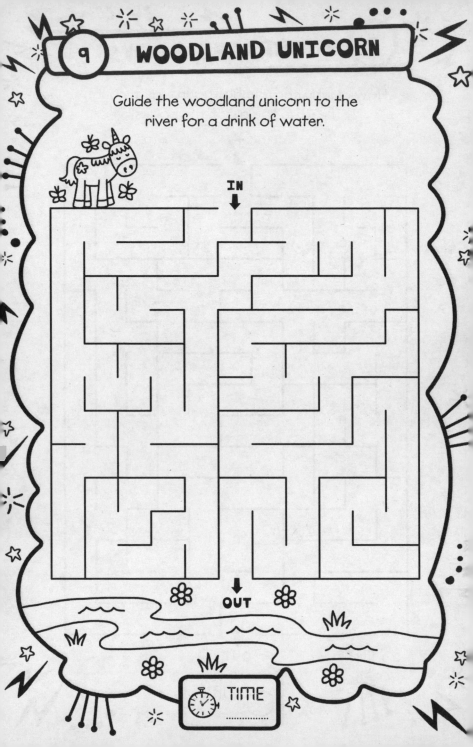

HOPPING AROUND

Take the frog to the middle of the maze to find the perfect lily pad to hop on.

IN

TIME

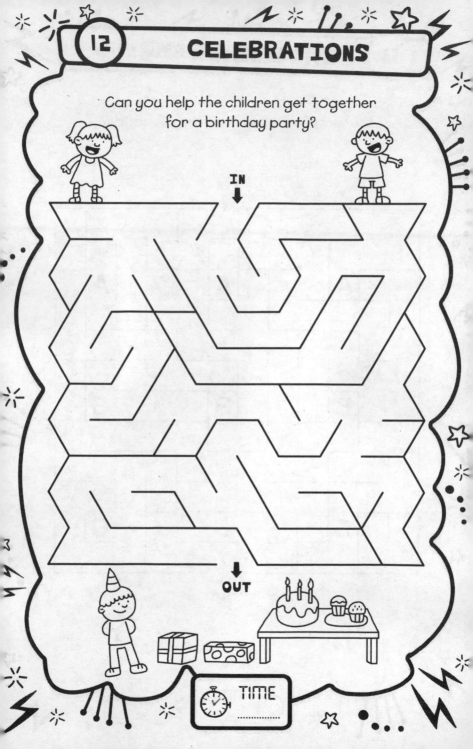

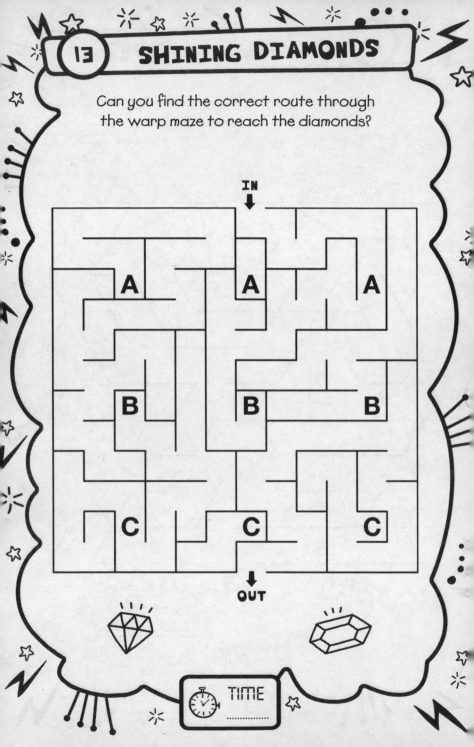

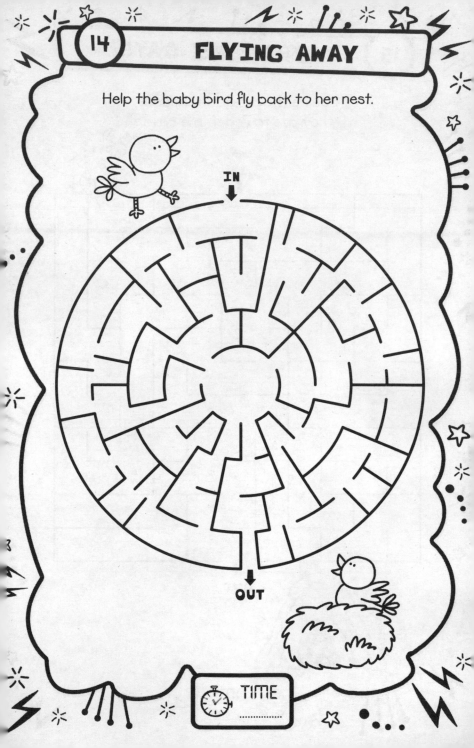

14 FLYING AWAY

Help the baby bird fly back to her nest.

IN

OUT

TIME

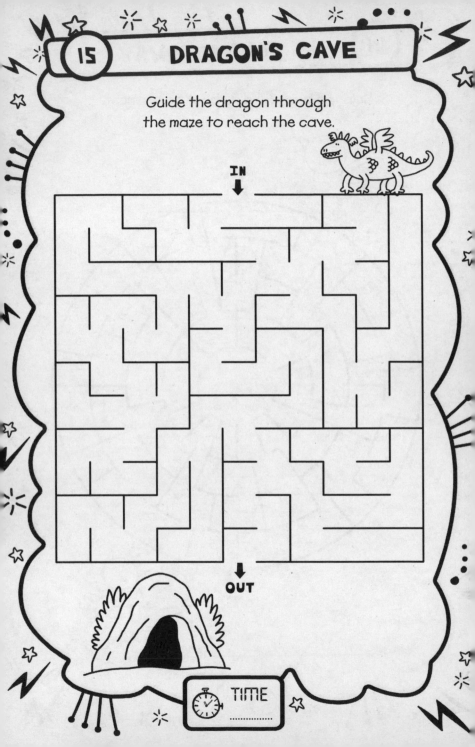

15 DRAGON'S CAVE

Guide the dragon through
the maze to reach the cave.

IN

OUT

TIME

MAGNIFYING GLASS

Can you find your way to
the middle of the maze?

IN

TIME
....

SHINING STAR

17

Guide the pentagon to the shining star.

IN

OUT

TIME

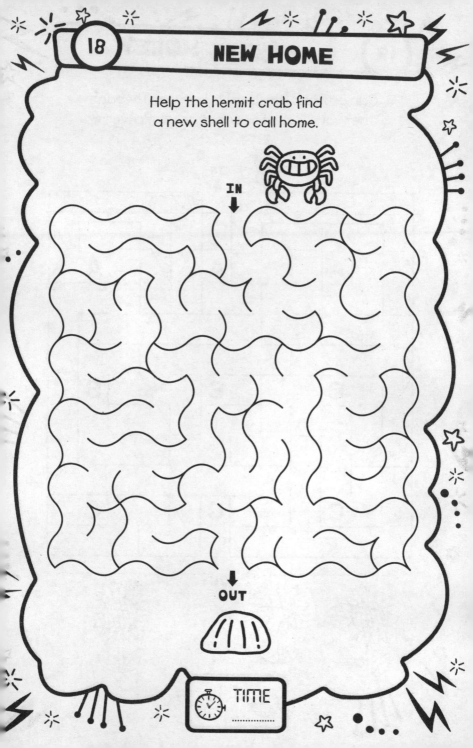

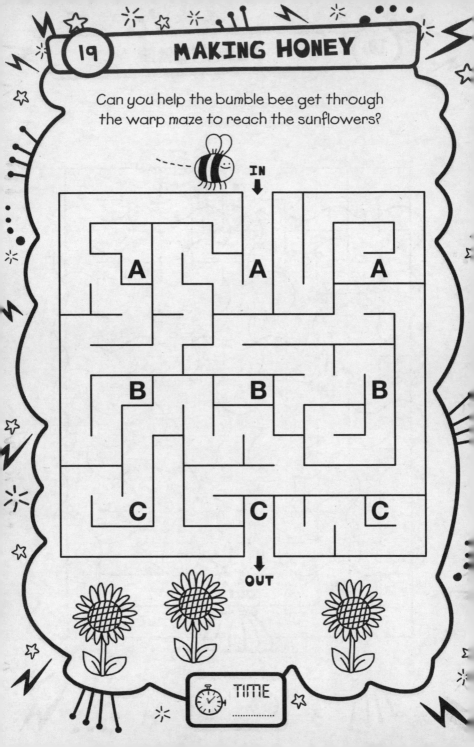

19 MAKING HONEY

Can you help the bumble bee get through the warp maze to reach the sunflowers?

IN

A A A

B B B

C C C

OUT

TIME

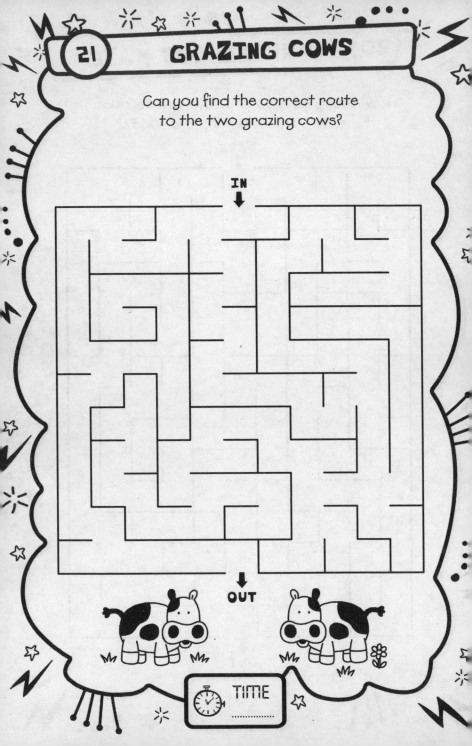

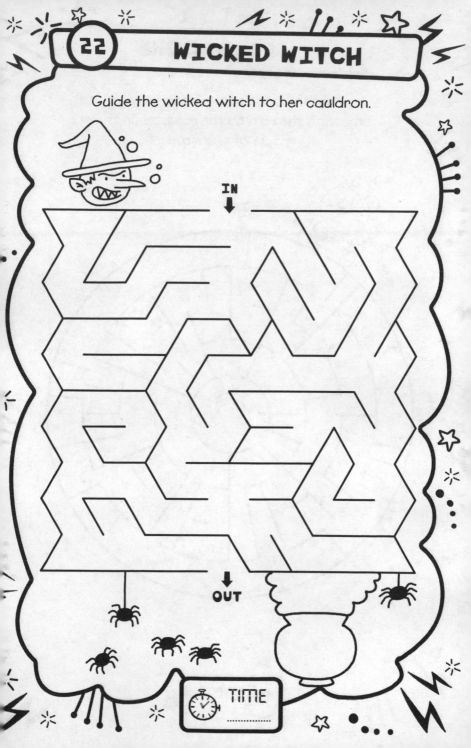

PANDACORN

Help the pandacorn find its way through the rain to the rainbow in the middle of the maze.

IN

TIME
....

How quickly can you travel through
the multi-floor maze?

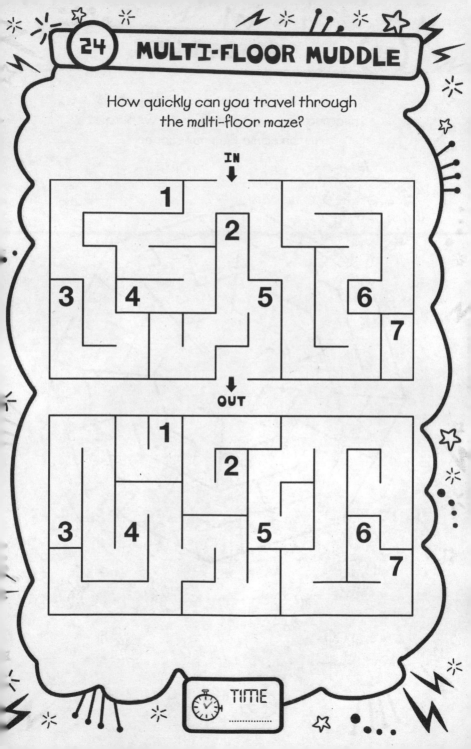

IN

1
2
3 4 5 6 7

OUT

1
2
3 4 5 6 7

TIME

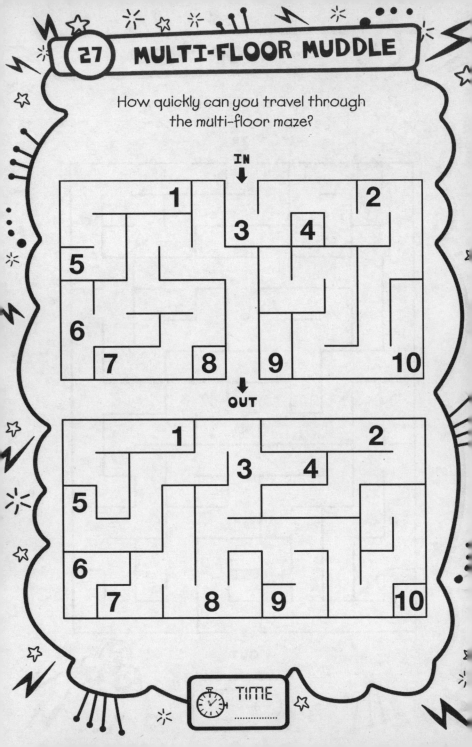

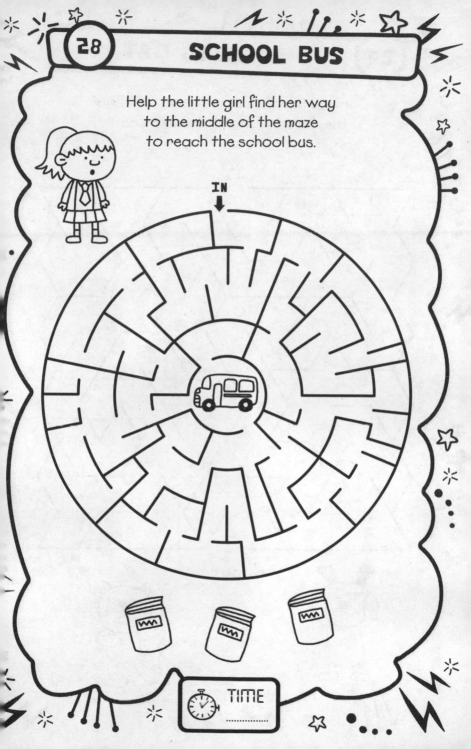

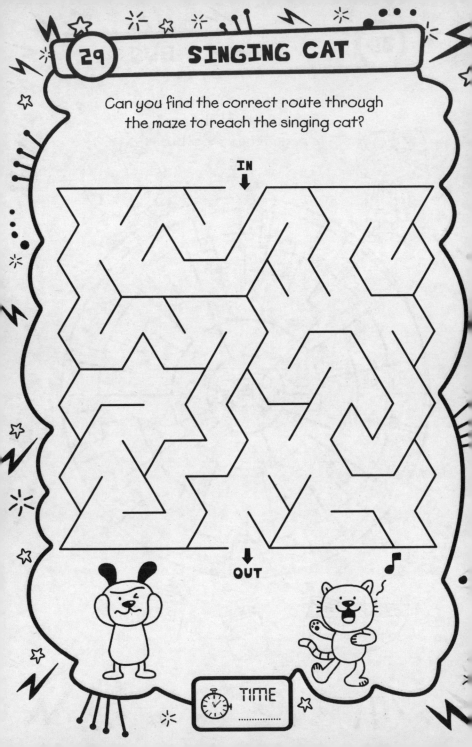

JUICY PEACH

The juicy peach needs to find its way to the fruit bowl.

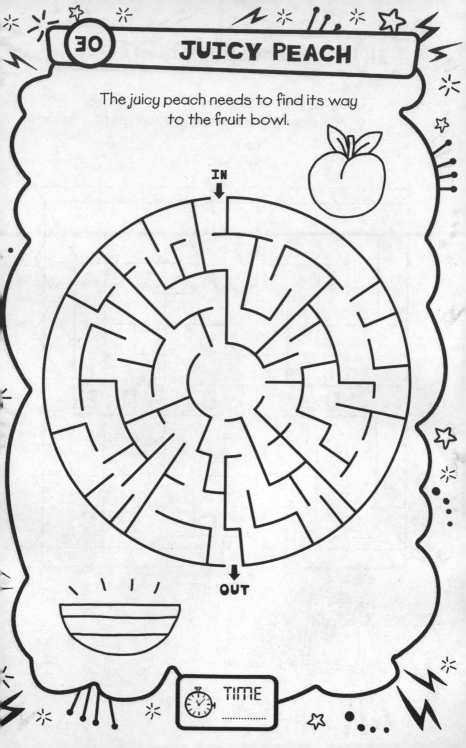

IN

OUT

TIME

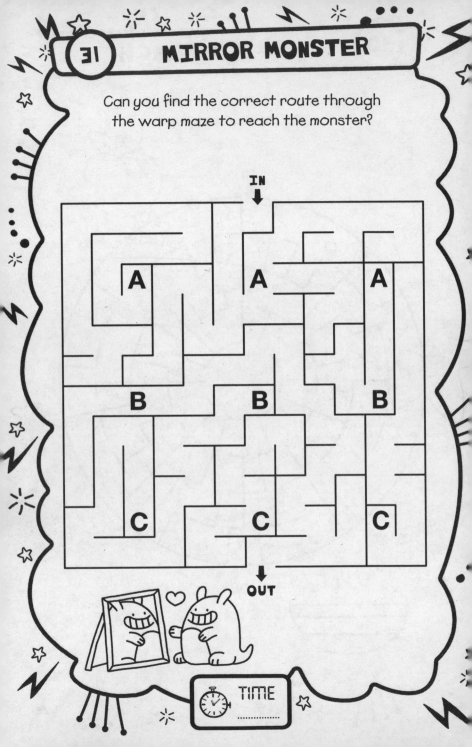

SHOOTING STAR

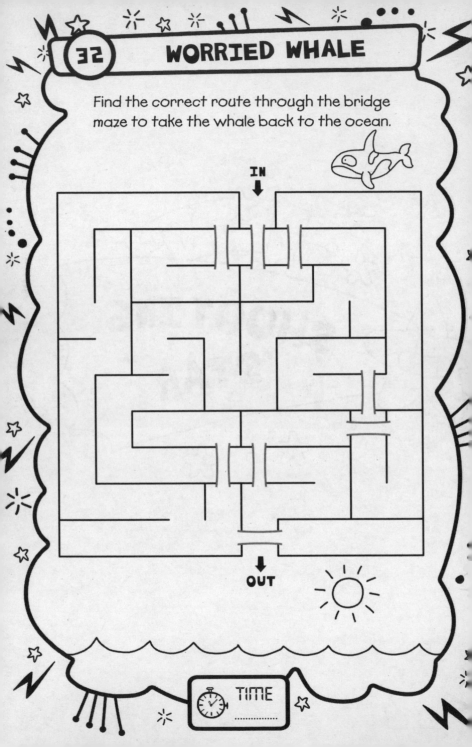

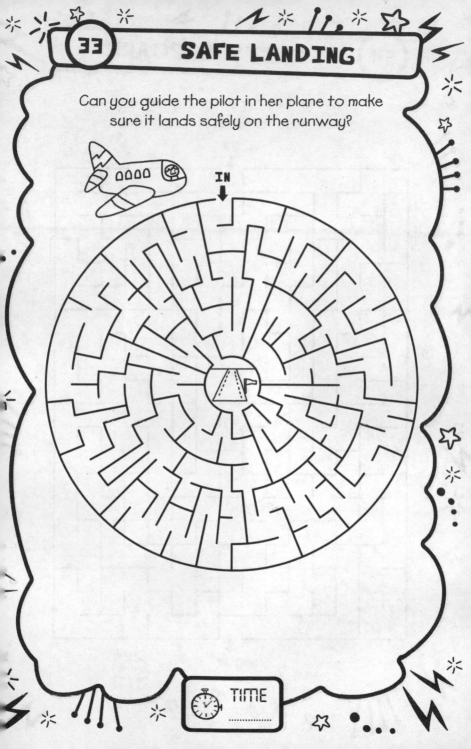

TASTY CUPCAKE

Follow the correct route through
the maze to reach the cupcake.

IN

OUT

TIME
....

CATCH A RIDE

Can you find the correct route through
the warp maze to catch a ride?

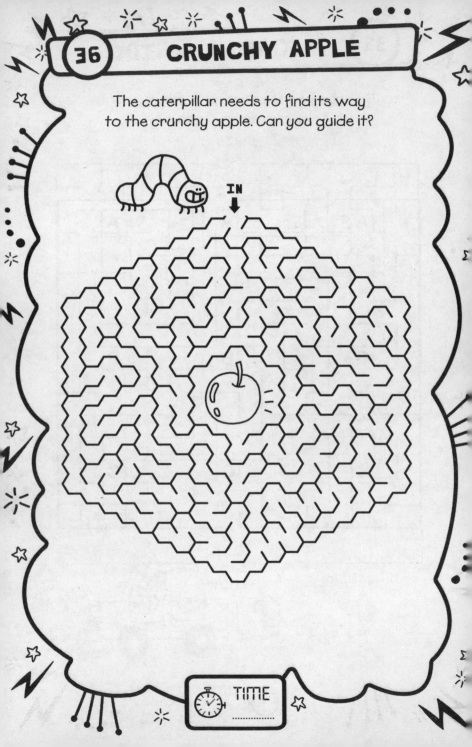

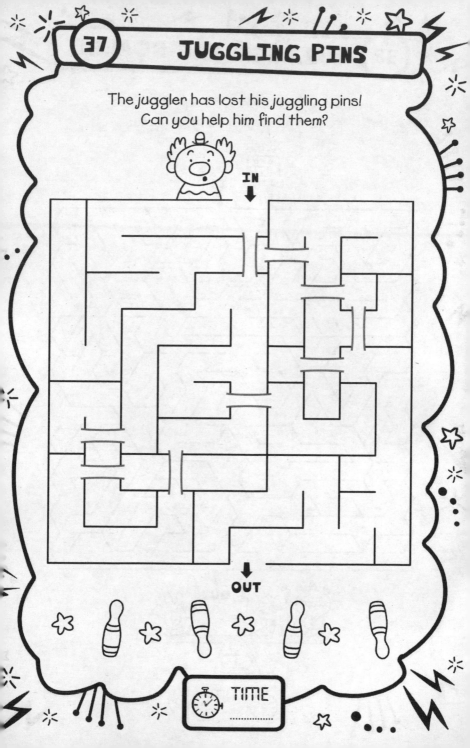

Guide the robot through the maze
to join his friends on the scales.

IN

OUT

TIME
....

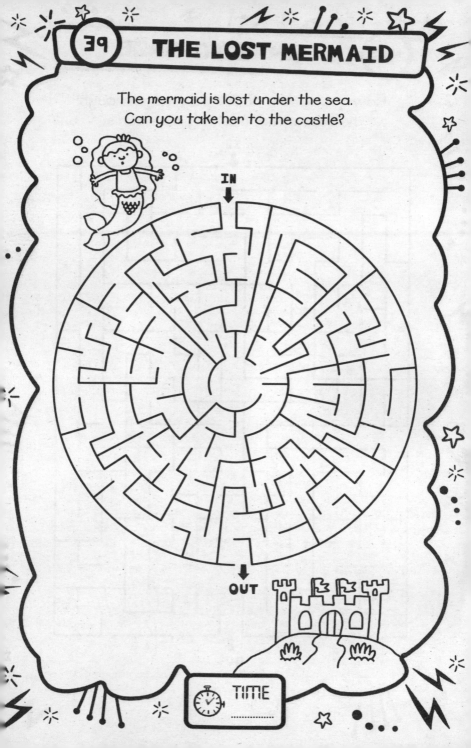

41 LOST FOOTBALL

Help the footballer find her lost football so that she can start the match.

IN

TIME
....

NOISY CATS

Follow the correct route through the maze. Beware of the noisy cats!

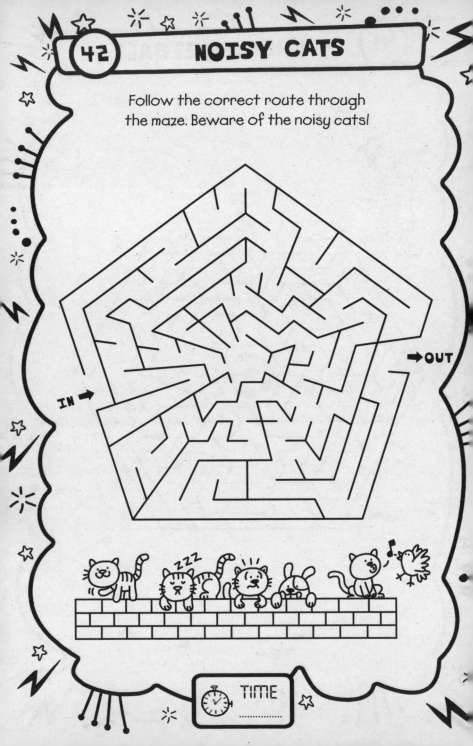

IN ➡

➡ OUT

TIME
....

CROWNING GLORY

Can you take the king through the maze to retrieve his crown?

IN

OUT

TIME
....

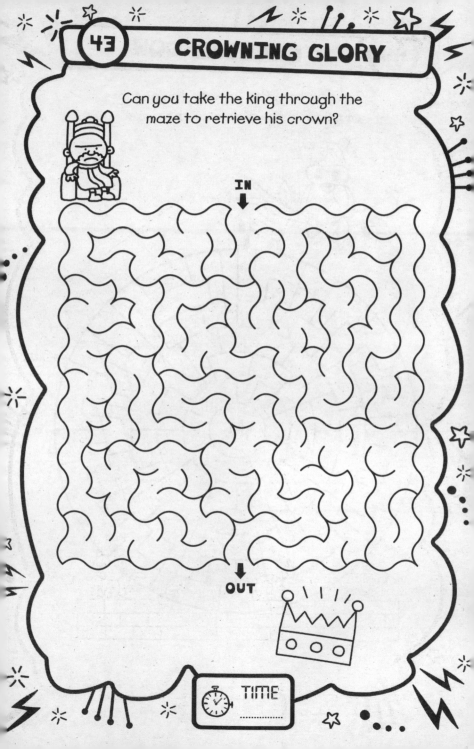

GRAZING COW

Can you take the cow to the patch of grass in the middle of the maze?

IN

TIME
....

TEST TUBES

The scientist needs to find her test tubes before she can finish the experiment. Can you help her reach them?

IN

OUT

TIME

ROW YOUR BOAT

Can you find the correct route through
the maze to reach the rowing boat?

IN

OUT

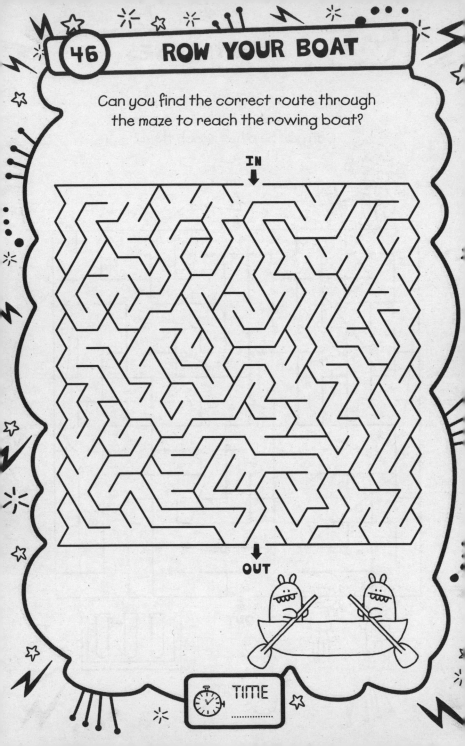

TIME

Take the clown through the maze
to reach his cluster of balloons.

IN ➡

➡ OUT

TIME

ALIEN SPACESHIP

Can you guide the baby alien through the bridge maze to reach the spaceship?

IN

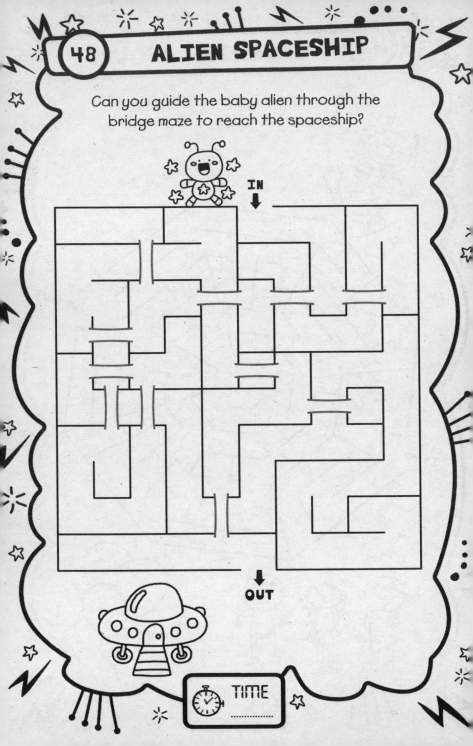

OUT

TIME

TOMATO CHASE

Can you find the correct route through the maze to join the tomato chase?

IN

OUT

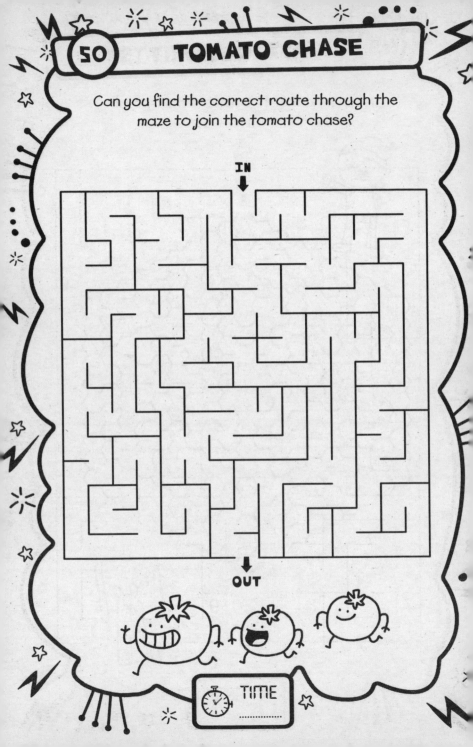

TIME
....

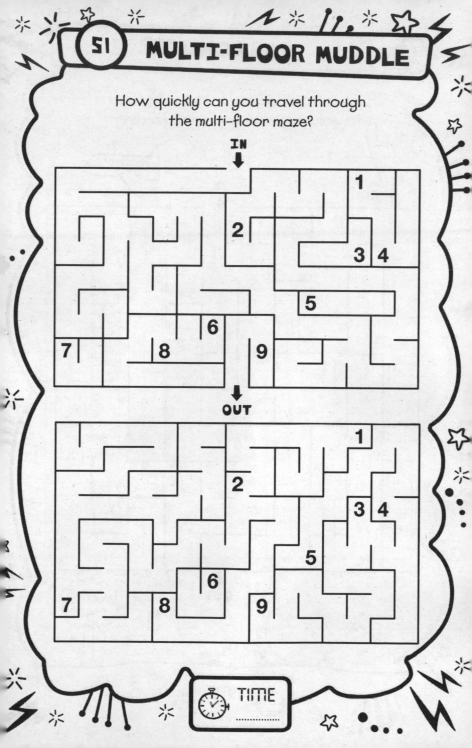

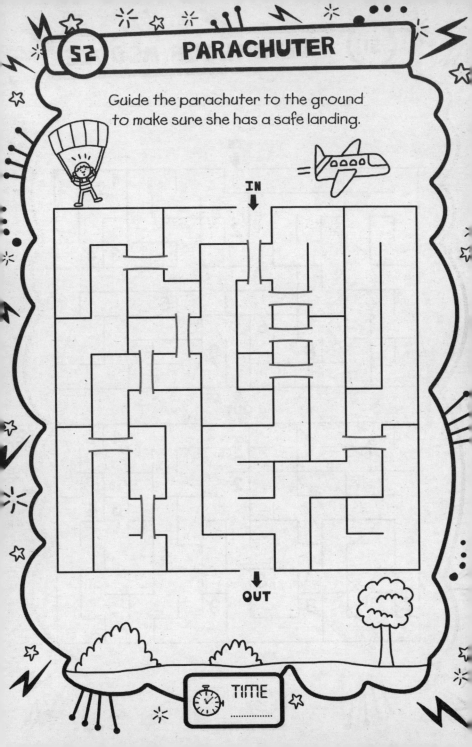

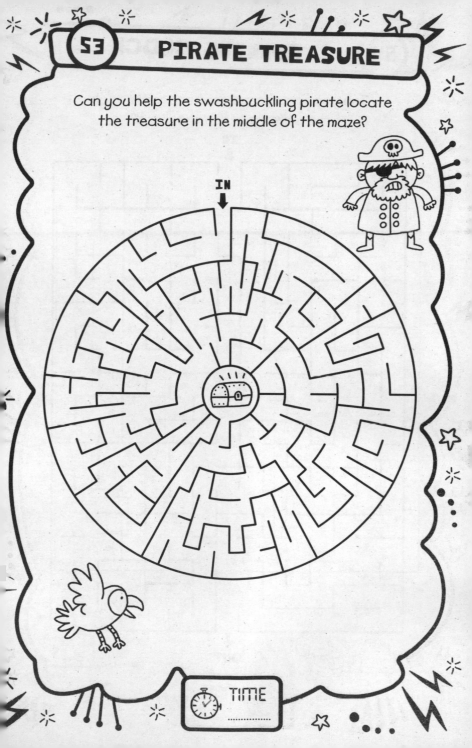

PIRATE TREASURE

Can you help the swashbuckling pirate locate the treasure in the middle of the maze?

IN

TIME
....

Can you find the correct route through the maze to reach the clock?

IN

OUT

TIME
....

MULTI-FLOOR MUDDLE

How quickly can you travel through
the multi-floor maze?

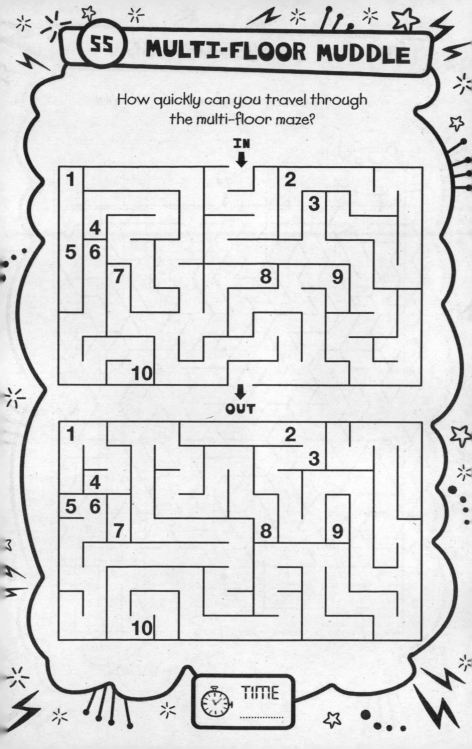

IN

1 2 3 4 5 6 7 8 9 10

OUT

TIME

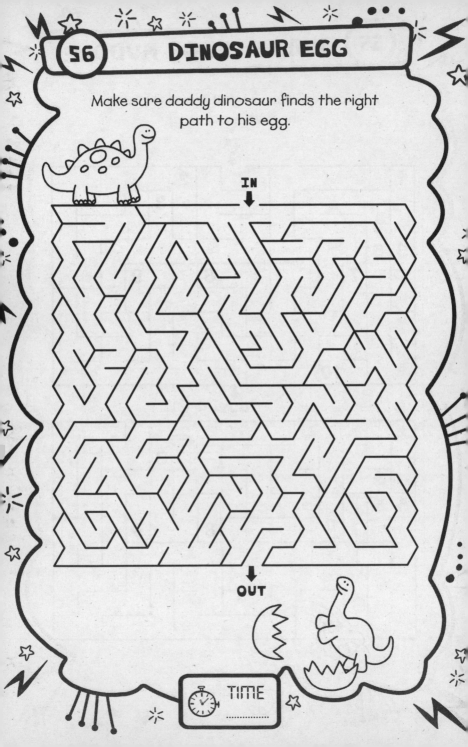

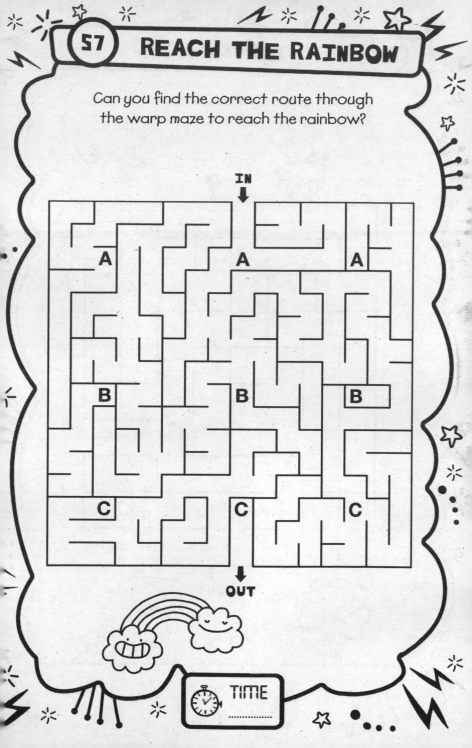

REACH THE RAINBOW

Can you find the correct route through
the warp maze to reach the rainbow?

IN

A   A   A

B   B   B

C   C   C

OUT

TIME

GUSTY WIND

Oh no! A gust of wind has blown the kite away. Can you help the little boy find it?

IN

OUT

TIME
....

TELESCOPE DISCOVERY

Can you find the correct route through
the warp maze to reach the telescope?

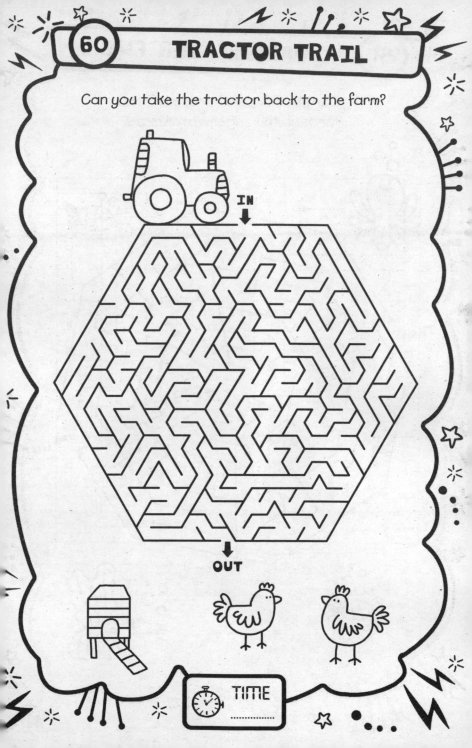

TIME FOR BED

Little rabbit is ready for bed. Help her find her way to the warm hutch.

IN

OUT

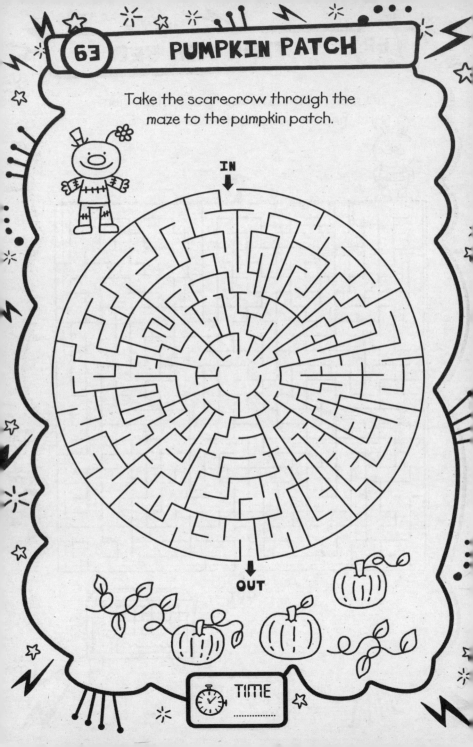

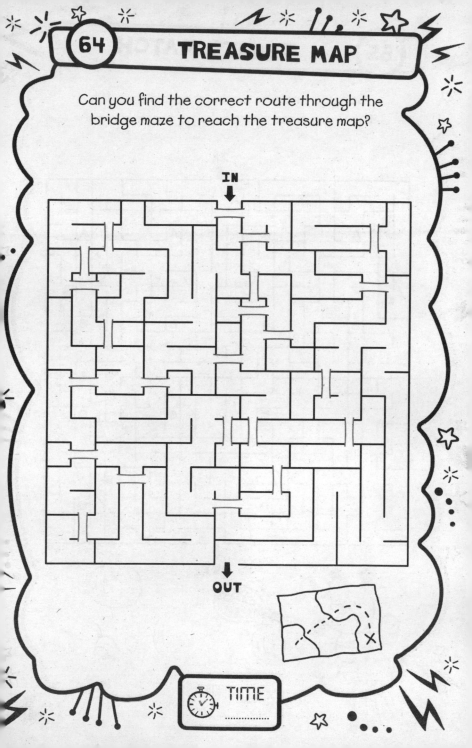

TREASURE MAP

Can you find the correct route through the
bridge maze to reach the treasure map?

IN

OUT

TIME

MOTHER HEN

Can you help the hen find her way back to
her clutch of eggs before they hatch?

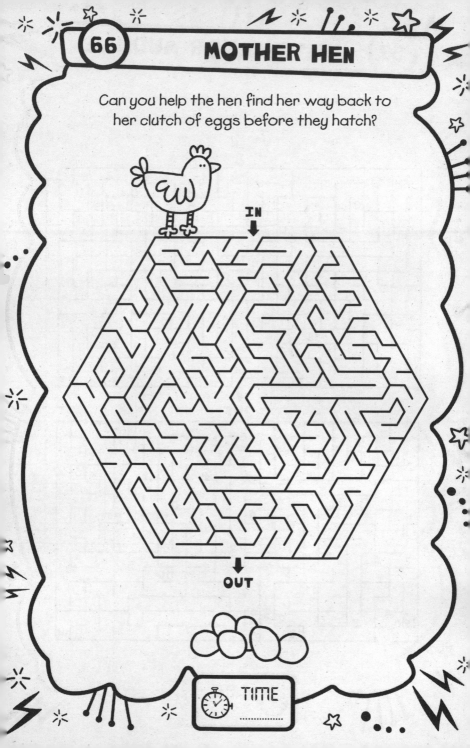

IN

OUT

TIME

MULTI-FLOOR MUDDLE

How quickly can you travel through
the multi-floor maze?

IN

OUT

TIME

....

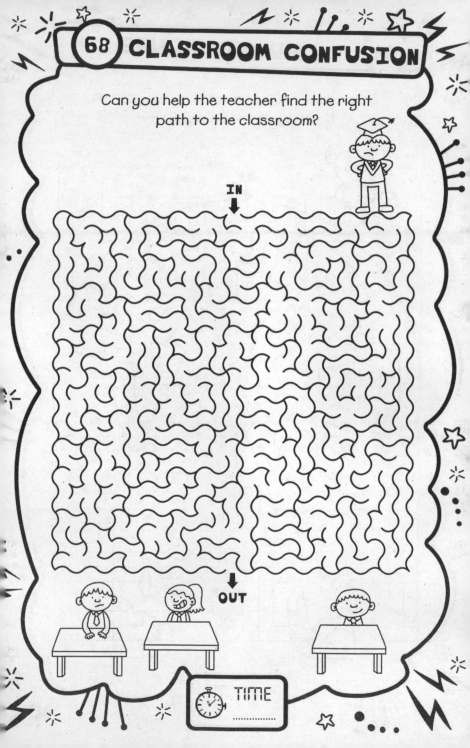

68 CLASSROOM CONFUSION

Can you help the teacher find the right path to the classroom?

IN

OUT

TIME

HUNGRY MOUSE

Help the hungry mouse follow his nose all the way to the smelly cheese.

SHAPE SHIFTER

Can you find the correct route
to the middle of the maze?

IN

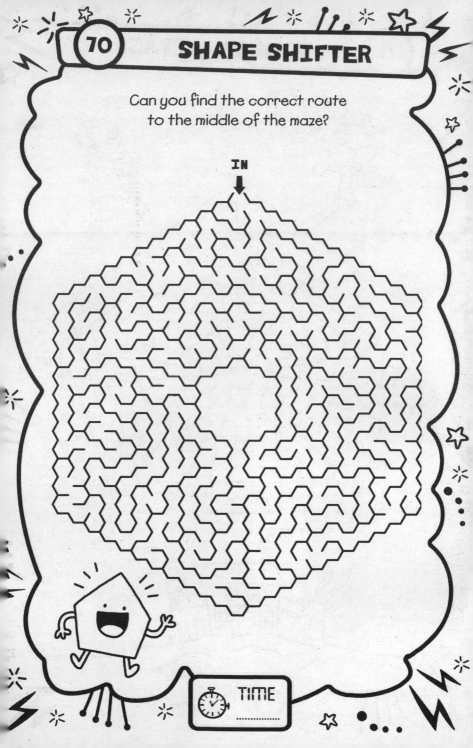

TIME

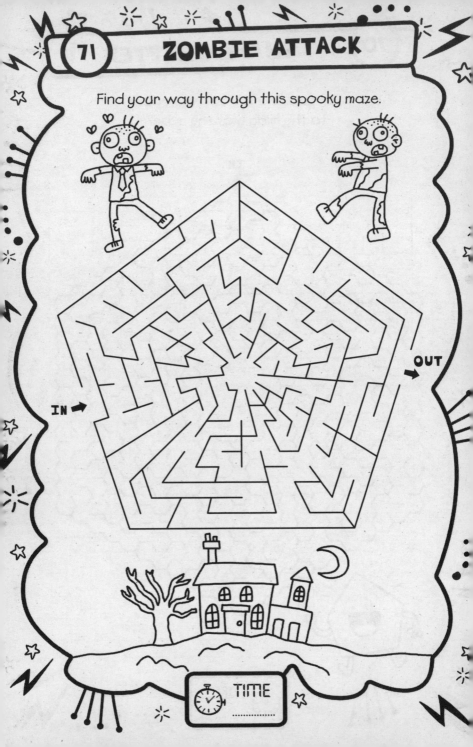

MULTI-FLOOR MUDDLE

How quickly can you travel through
the multi-floor maze?

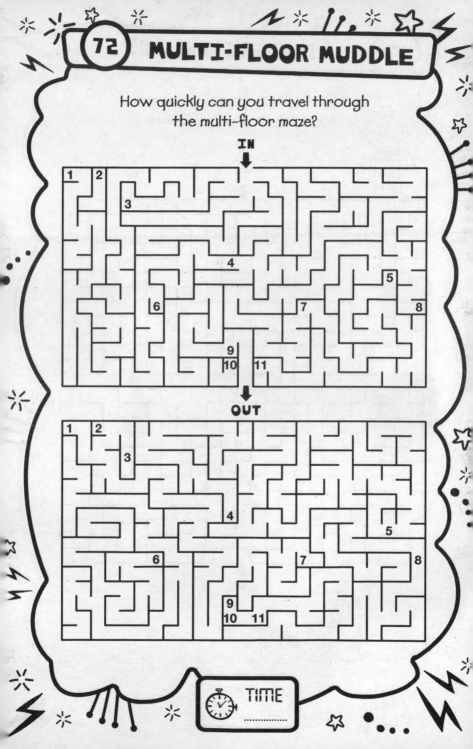

DESERT ISLAND

Guide the sailor through the maze
to reach the desert island.

IN

OUT

TIME

CREATURE CAKE

Can you take the creature to the
cake in the middle of the maze?

IN

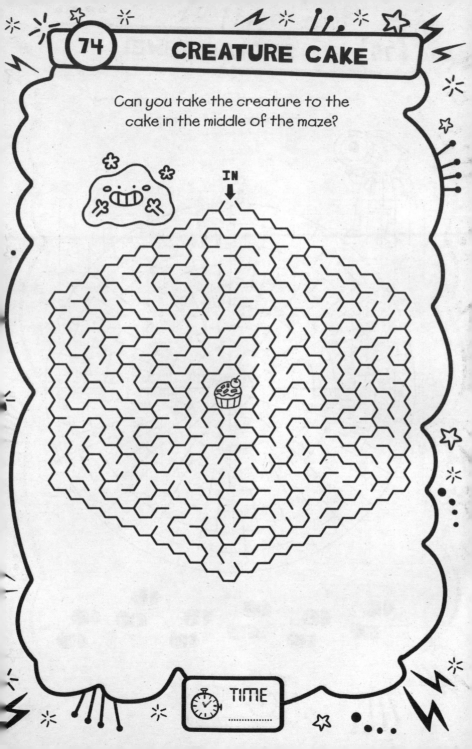

BUZZING AROUND

Can you guide the bees through
the maze to reach their home?

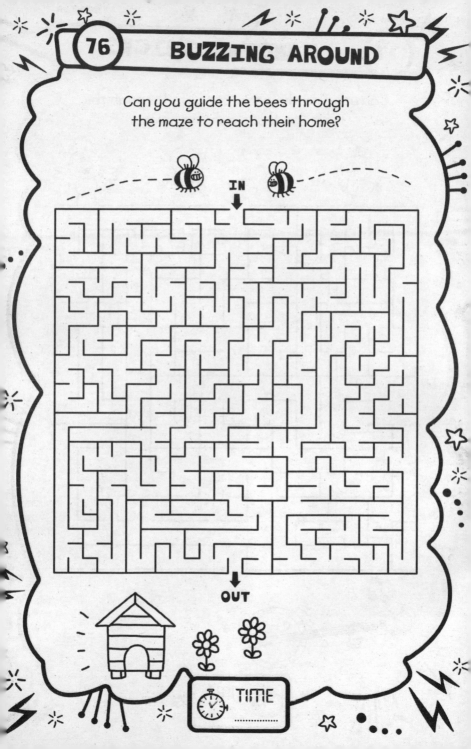

IN

OUT

TIME

DANCING CHICKS

Can you find the correct route through the
maze for these dancing chicks?

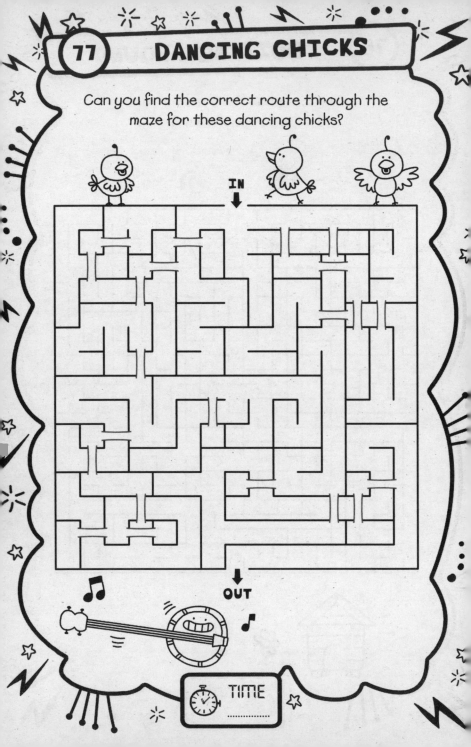

PENTAGON PLANET

Guide the alien through the pentagon planet maze.

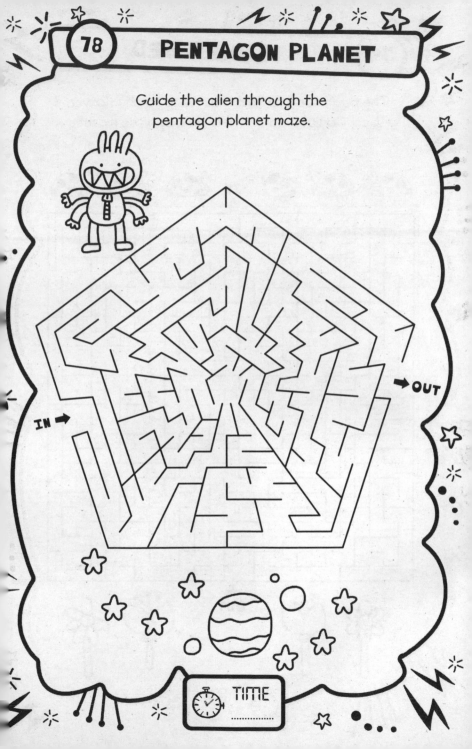

IN →

→ OUT

TIME

WINGING IT

Take the bat through the maze to his friend.

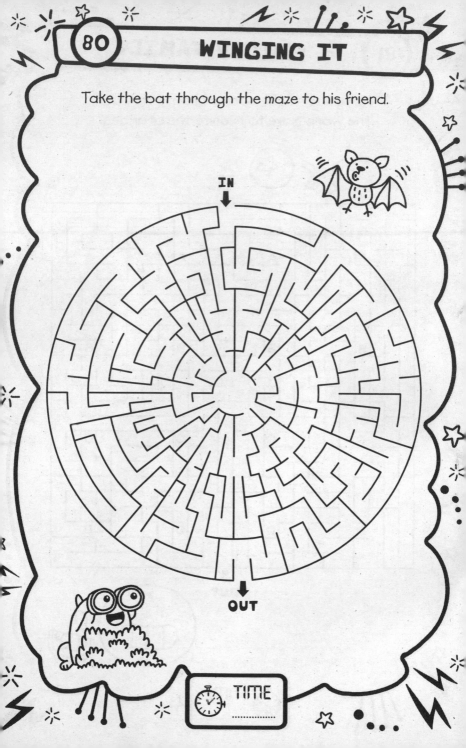

IN

OUT

TIME

FRUITY FAMILY

81

Can you find the correct route through the warp maze to reunite the oranges?

IN

OUT

TIME

HUNGRY MONKEY

Help the little lost monkey find
his way back to his banana.

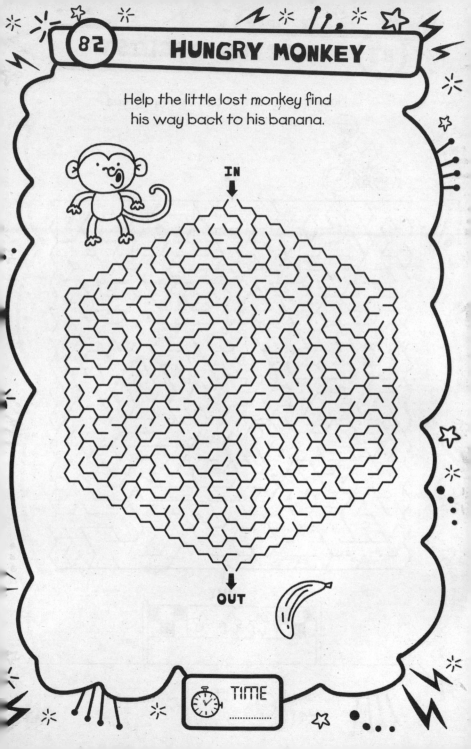

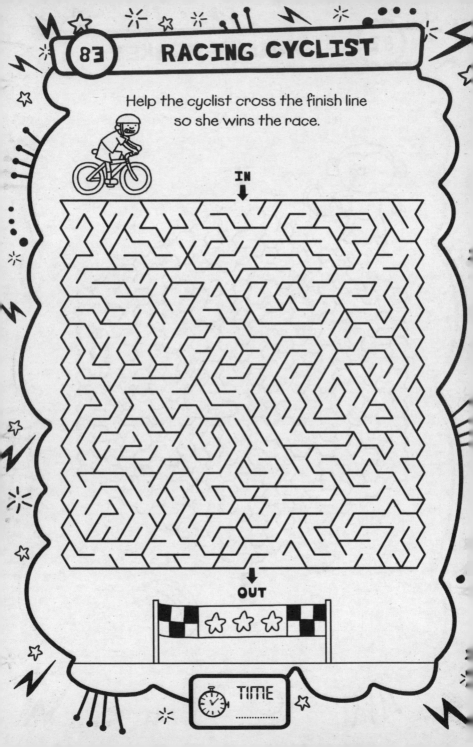

FALLING LEAVES

How quickly can you get to the middle
of the maze and reach the acorn?

IN

TIME

LITTLE CHICK

Can you take this little chick through the maze without getting in a muddle?

IN

OUT

TIME
....

MULTI-FLOOR MUDDLE

How quickly can you travel through
the multi-floor maze?

IN

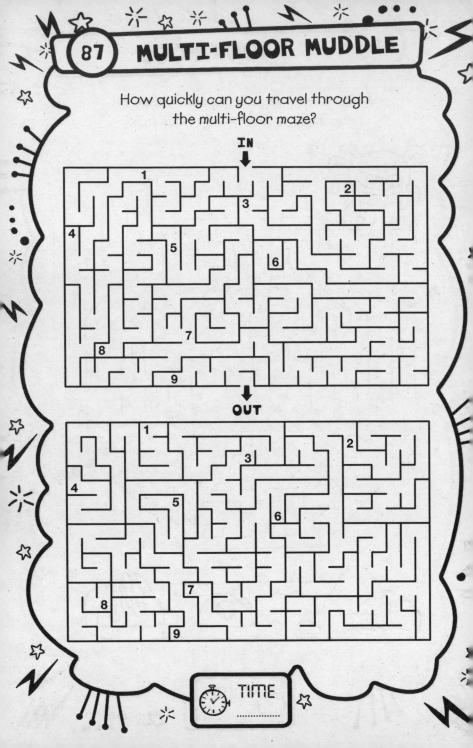

OUT

TIME
....

STARGAZER

Guide the astronomer to her telescope so she can stargaze.

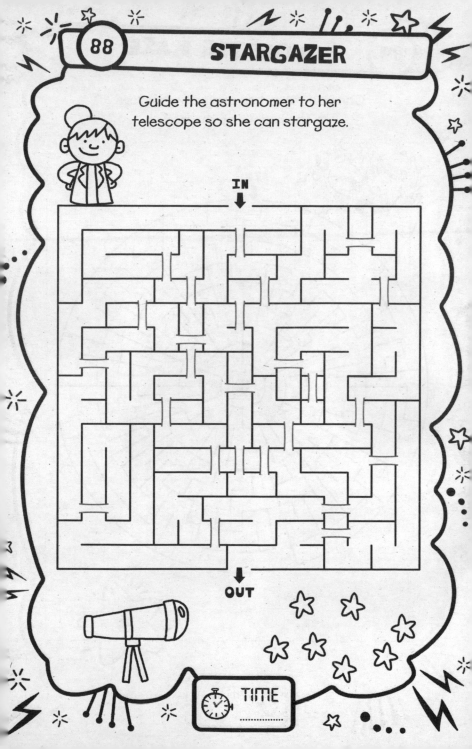

IN

OUT

TIME

MONSTER MAZE

Can you take the family of monsters
to the middle of the maze?

IN

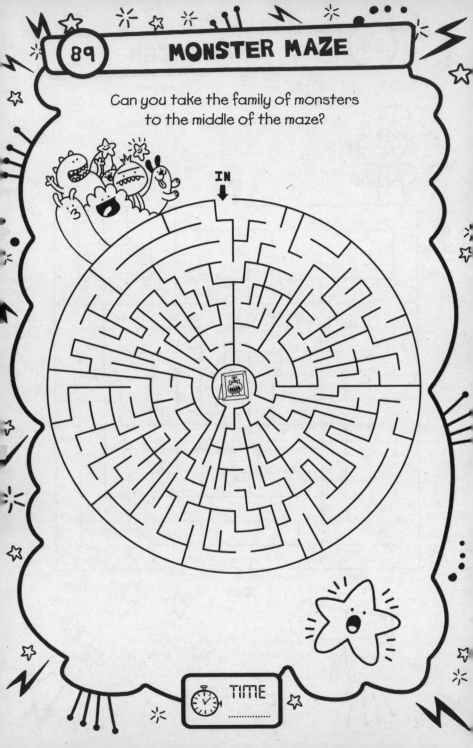

TIME
....

LETTER BOX

Make sure the letter gets posted in the letter box at the end of the maze.

IN

OUT

TIME
....

MULTI-FLOOR MUDDLE

How quickly can you travel through
the multi-floor maze?

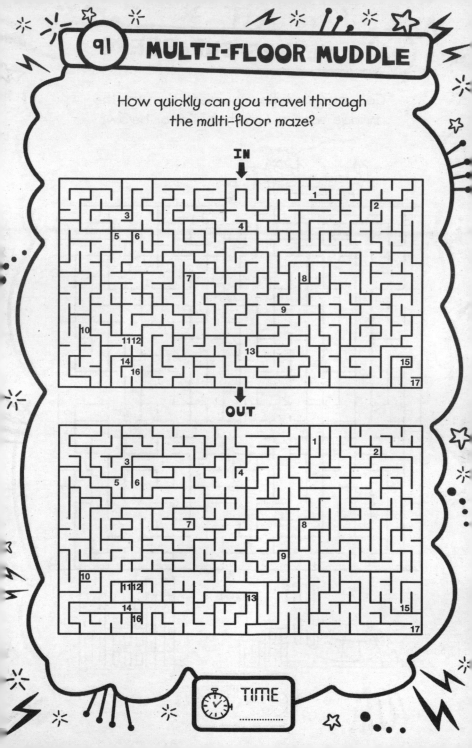

TIME
....

FLYING SUPERHERO

Can you guide the superhero through the bridge maze and to the buildings below?

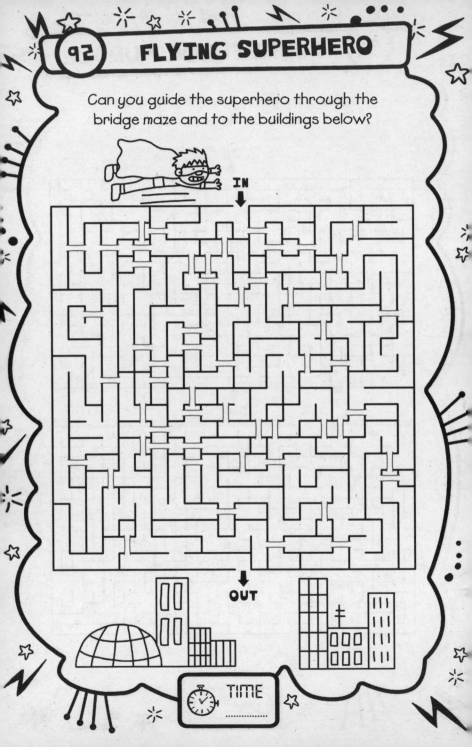

IN

OUT

TIME

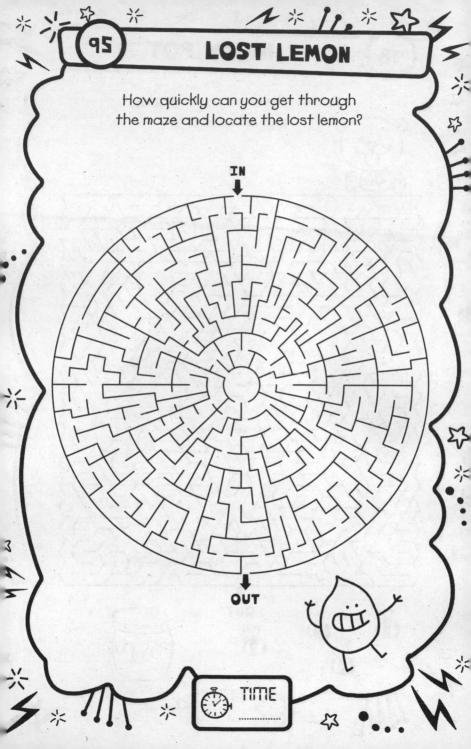

LOST LEMON

How quickly can you get through
the maze and locate the lost lemon?

IN

OUT

TIME

HONEY POT

Take the bear to the delicious pot of honey.

IN

OUT

TIME
....

Can you help the diver through
the maze to reach the submarine?

IN

OUT

TIME
....

CRAZY ALIENS

Can you help the alien through
the maze to join the others?

IN

OUT

TIME

FARM FRIENDS

How quickly can you guide the
sheep to the middle of the maze?

IN

TIME

MIND-BOGGLING

Can you find the correct route
through this mind-boggling maze?

IN

OUT

TIME
....

SLITHERING SNAKE

Find the correct route to take the snake through the bridge maze.

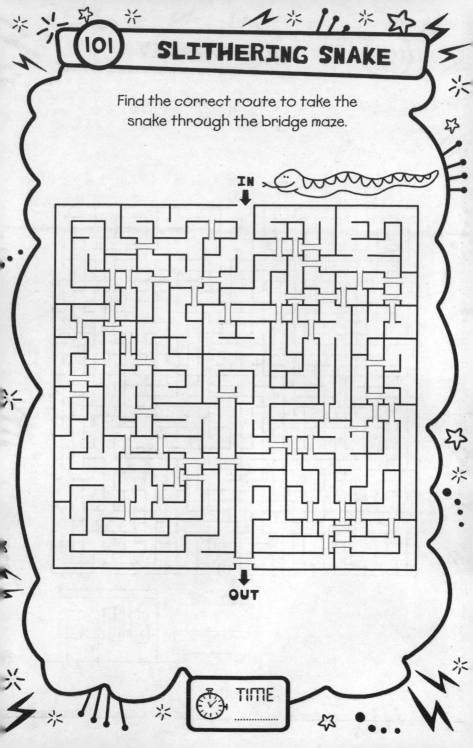

IN

OUT

TIME

ROCK CLIMBER

Guide the rock climber through the correct path to the top of the mountain.

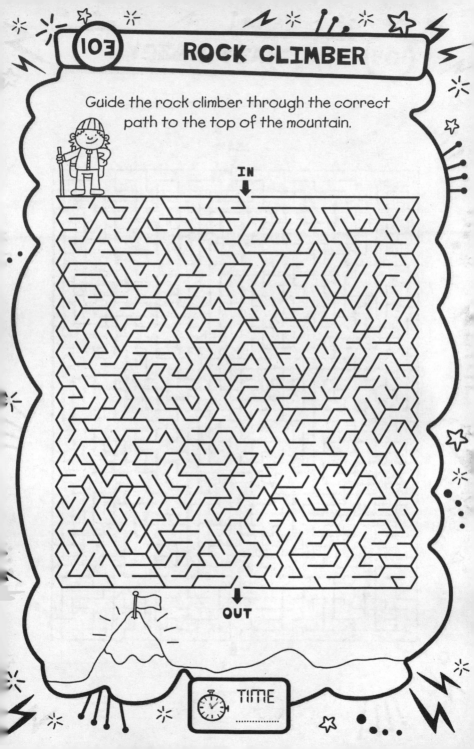

IN

OUT

TIME

CRAZY MAZEY

Can you find your way through the maze
without getting in a muddle?

IN

OUT

TIME
....

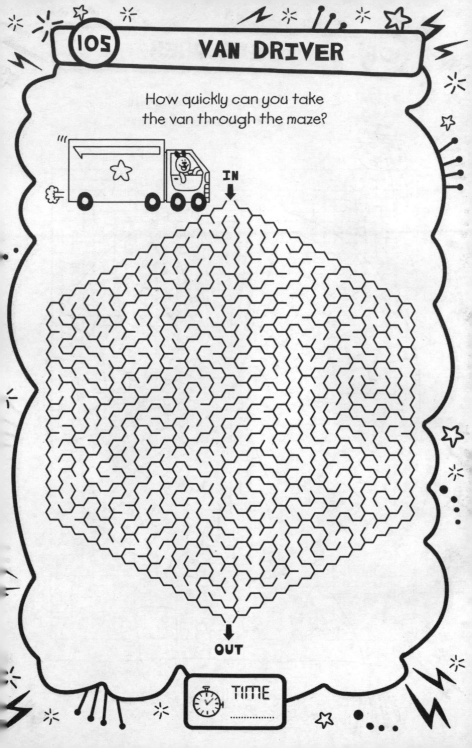

EXPLORER

Take the explorer back to his tent in the middle of the maze.

IN

TIME

TRAIN CONDUCTOR

Help the train conductor find her way back to the passengers.

IN

OUT

TIME

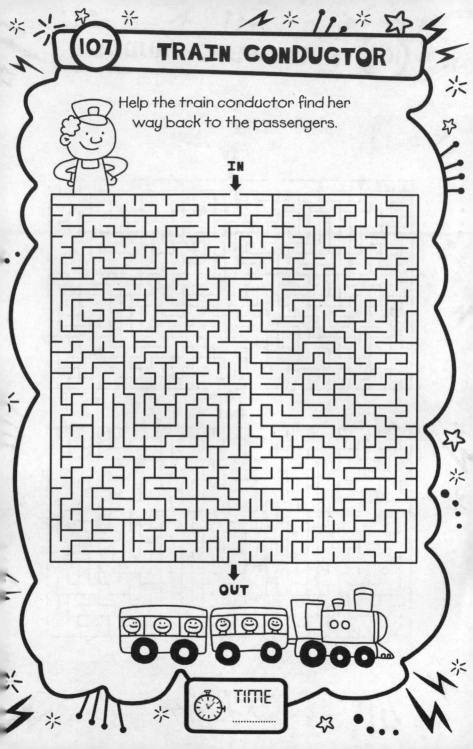

WINNER'S TROPHY

Help the athlete to the podium
to collect her trophy.

IN

OUT

TIME
....

SHARK ATTACK

112

Find the correct route to the middle of the maze and avoid the shark attack.

IN

TIME

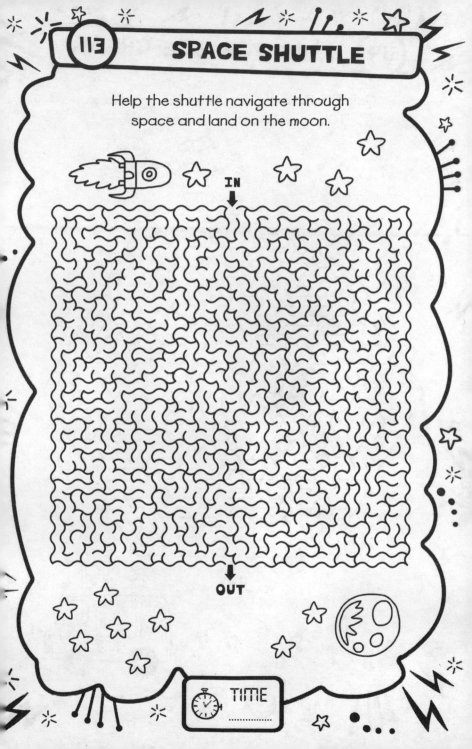

SPACE SHUTTLE

Help the shuttle navigate through space and land on the moon.

IN

OUT

TIME

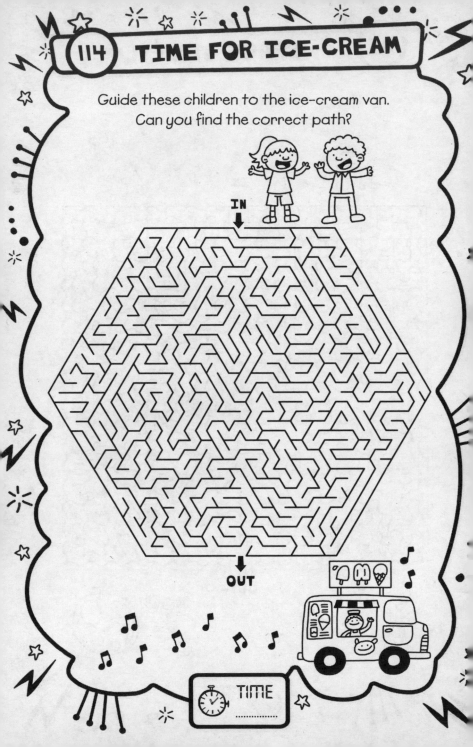

HUNGRY SQUIRREL

Guide the squirrel to the acorn
in the middle of the maze.

IN

TIME

SCARY MONSTER

Can you find the correct route through the monster's maze?

IN →

→ OUT

TIME
....

118 CUNNING CROCODILE

Help the cunning crocodile find his way back to the murky swamp.

IN

OUT

TIME

BOOK BOGGLE

Can you guide the librarian through
the maze to reach his books?

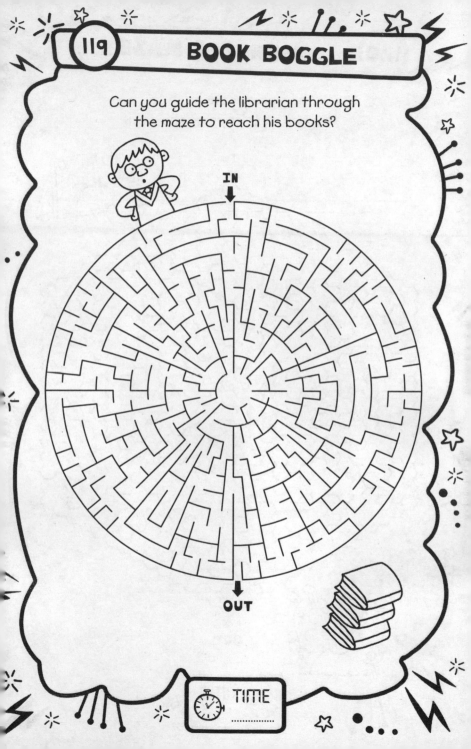

IN

OUT

TIME
....

MONSTER MAZE

Guide the monster through the maze
toward its friends on the rock.

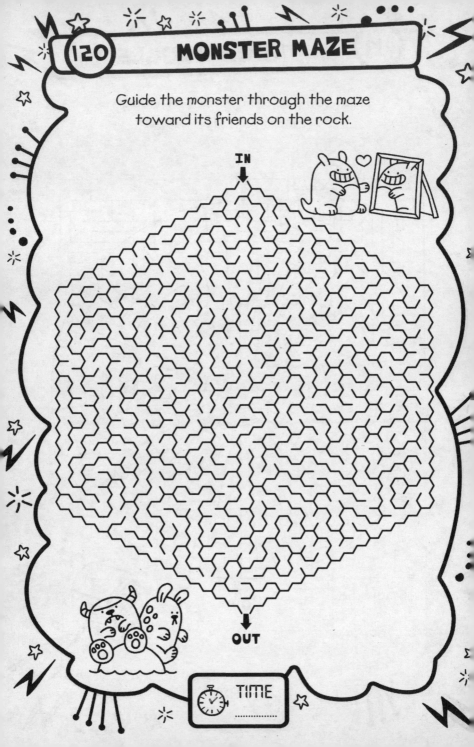

IN

OUT

TIME

ALL THE
ANSWERS

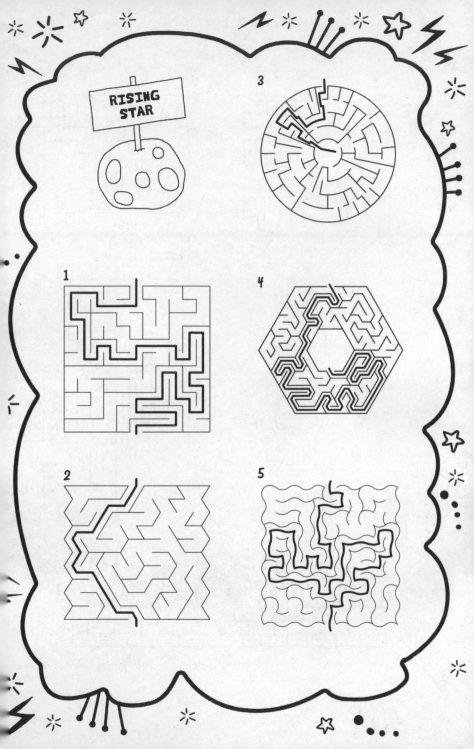

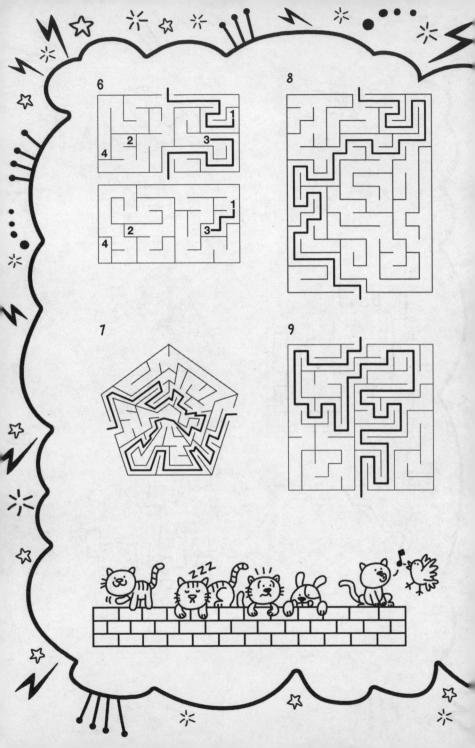

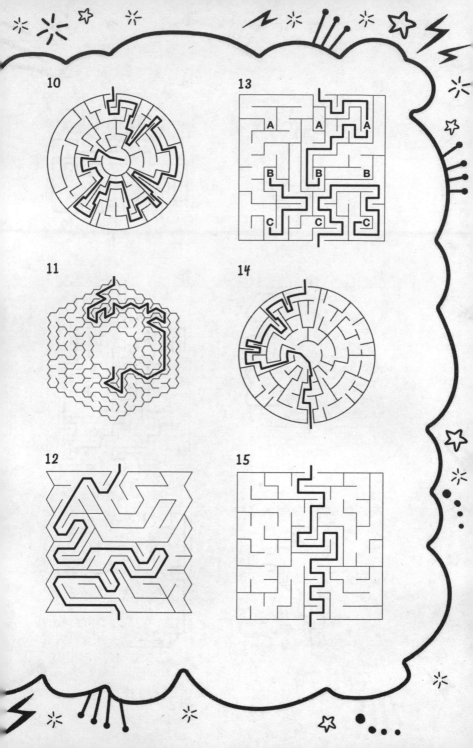

10

13

11

14

12

15

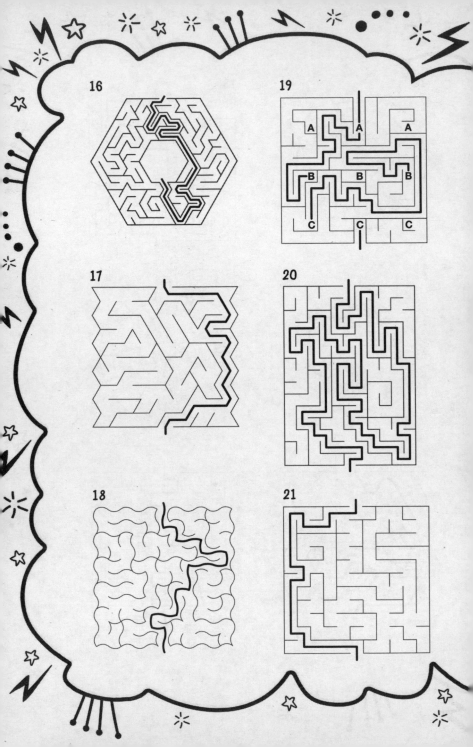

16

19

17

20

18

21

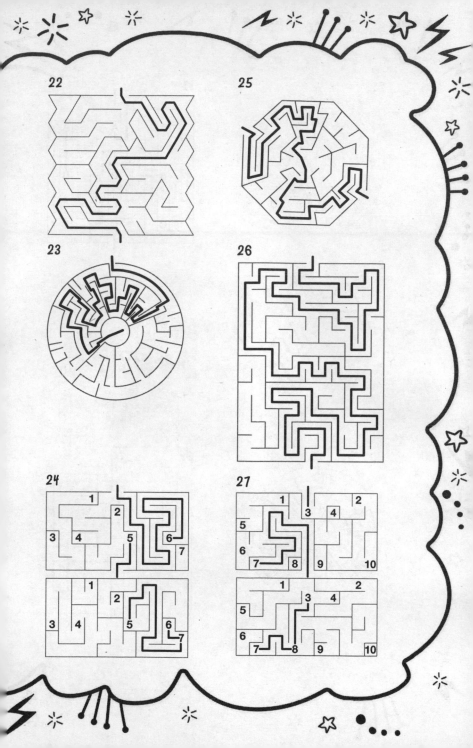

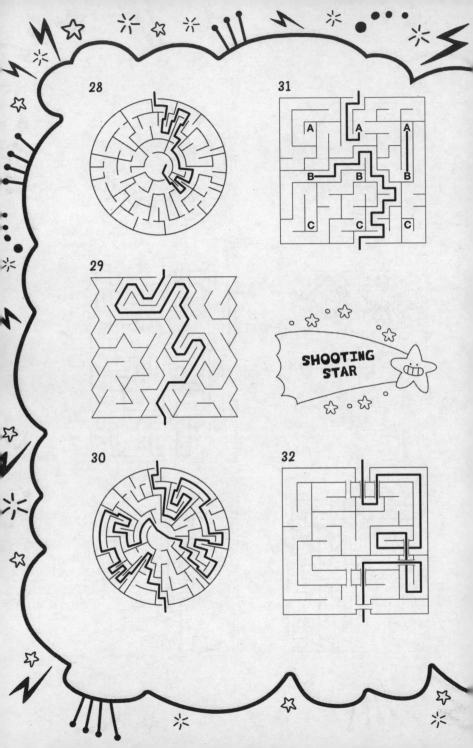

28

31

A   A   A

B   B   B

C   C   C

29

SHOOTING STAR

30

32

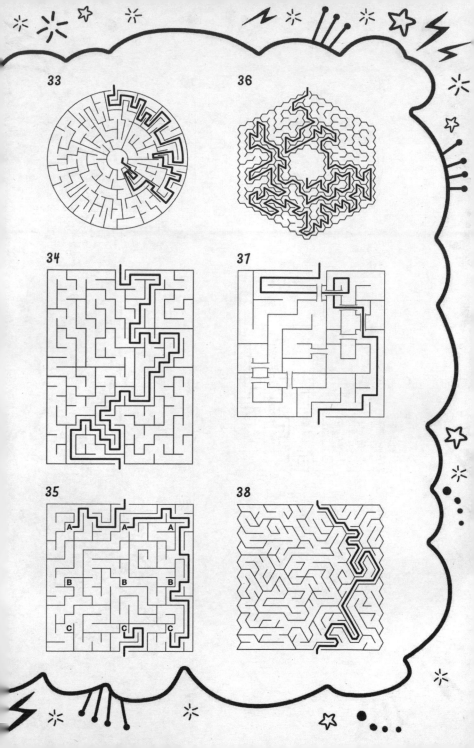

33

36

34

37

35

A · A · A
B · B · B
C · C · C

38

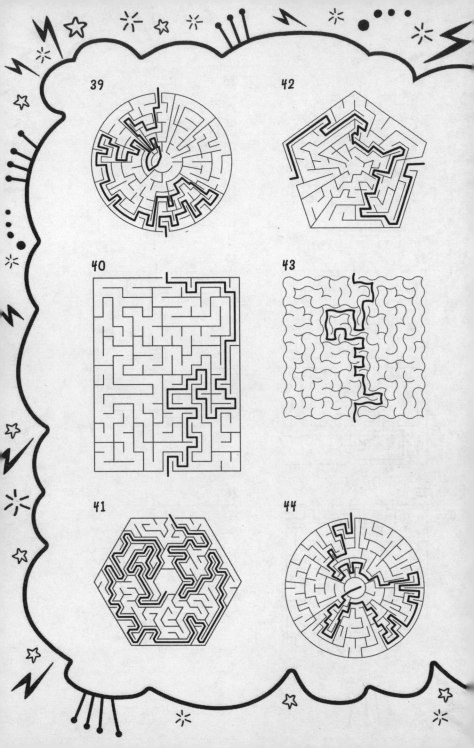

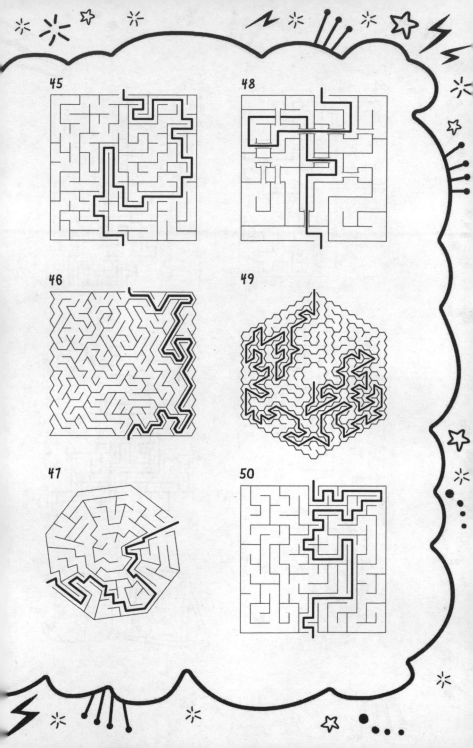

45

46

47

48

49

50

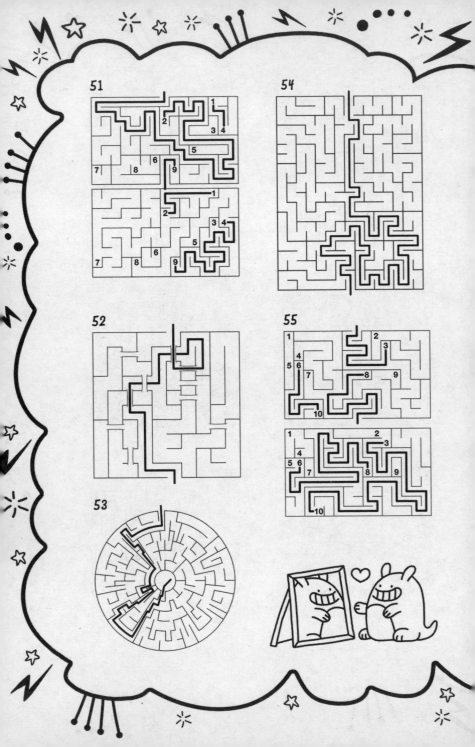

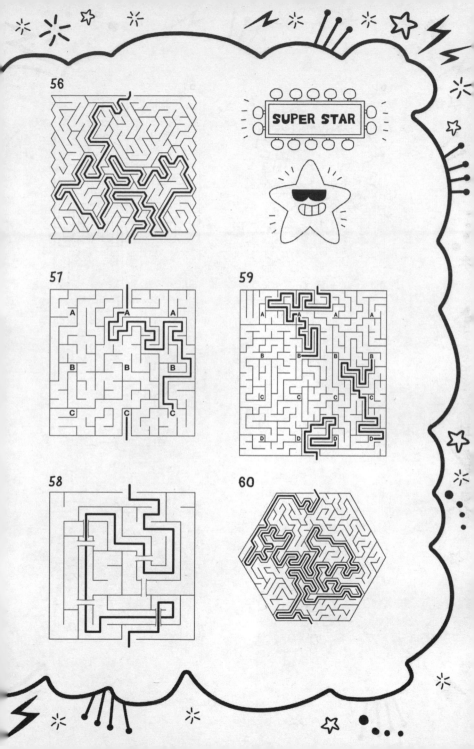

56

SUPER STAR

57

59

58

60

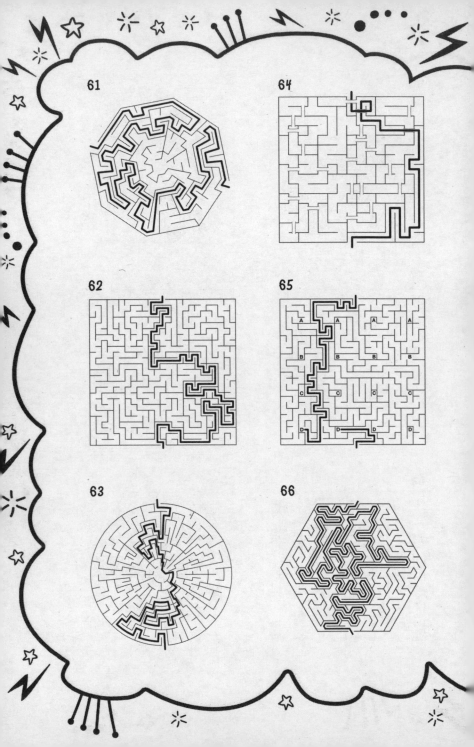

61

64

62

65

63

66

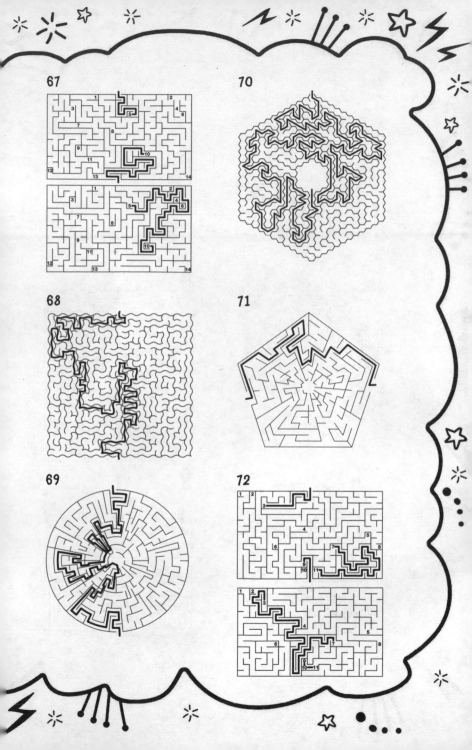

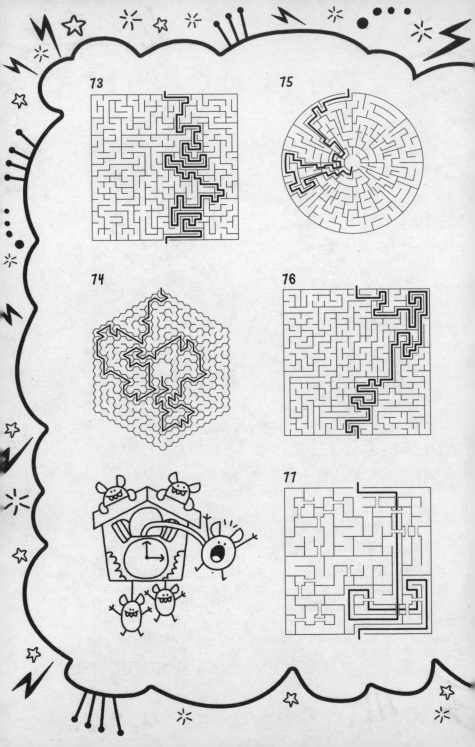

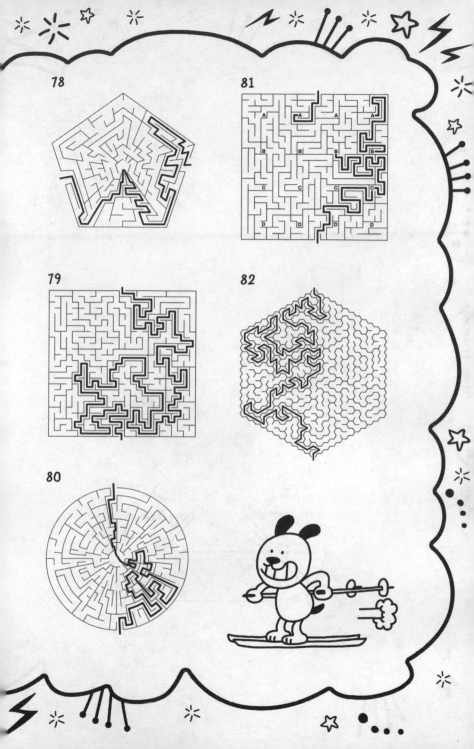

78

81

79

82

80

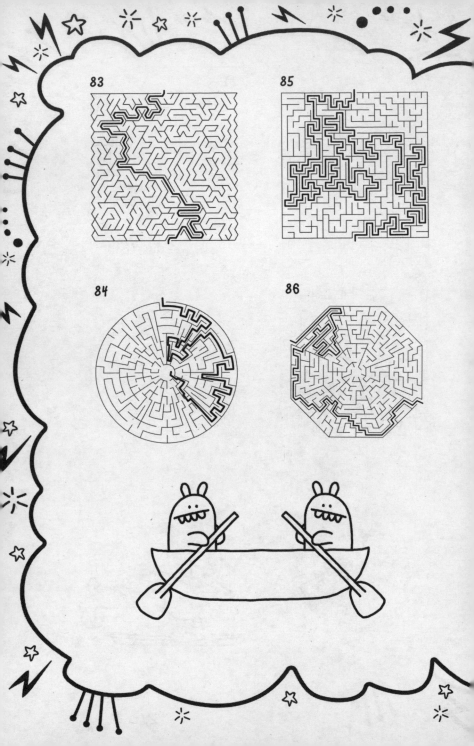

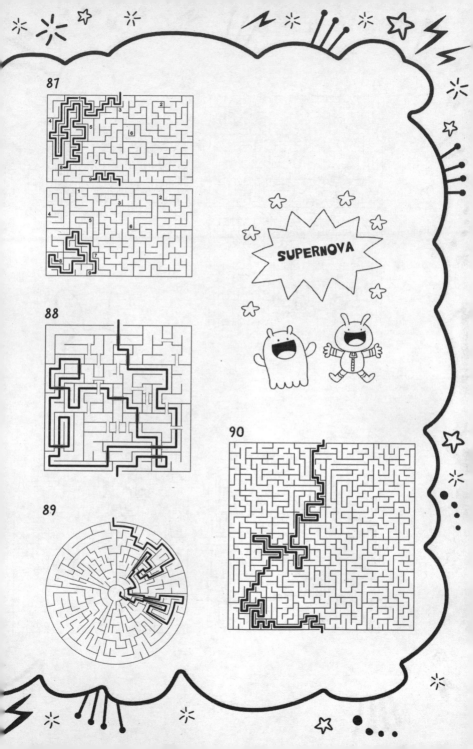

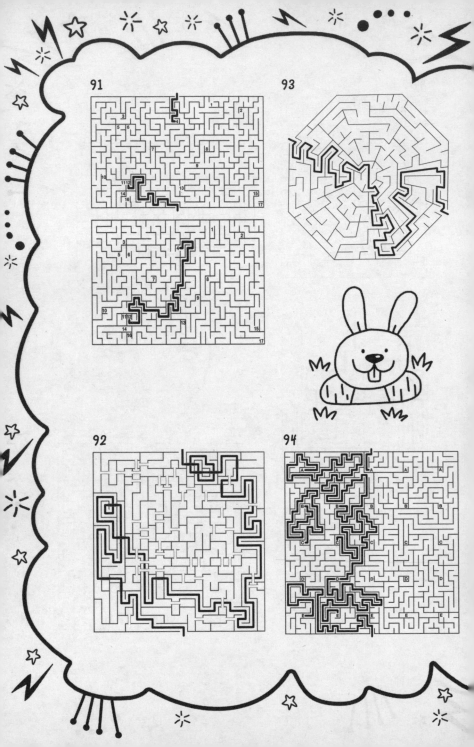

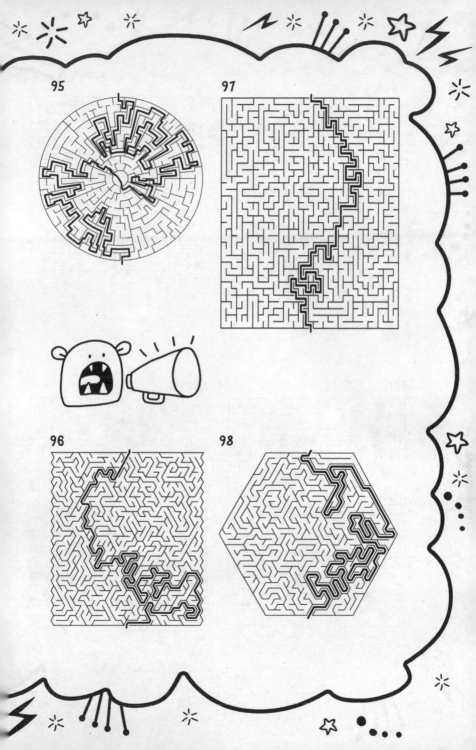

95

97

96

98

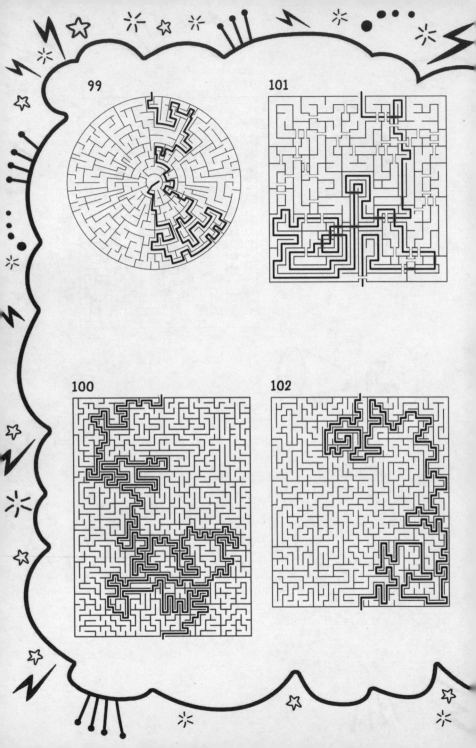

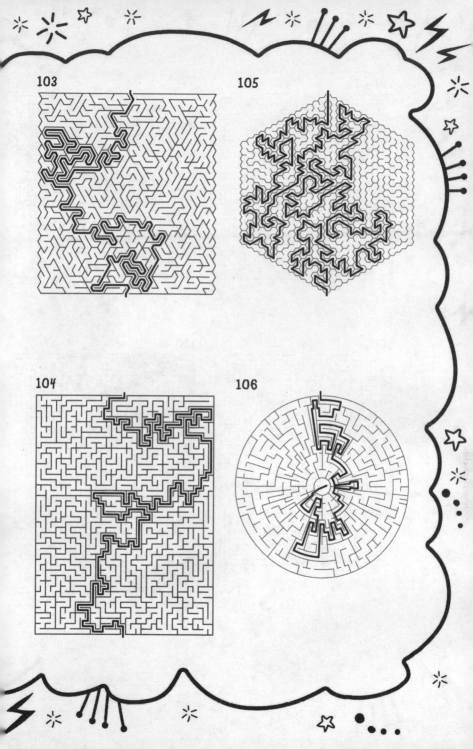

103

105

104

106

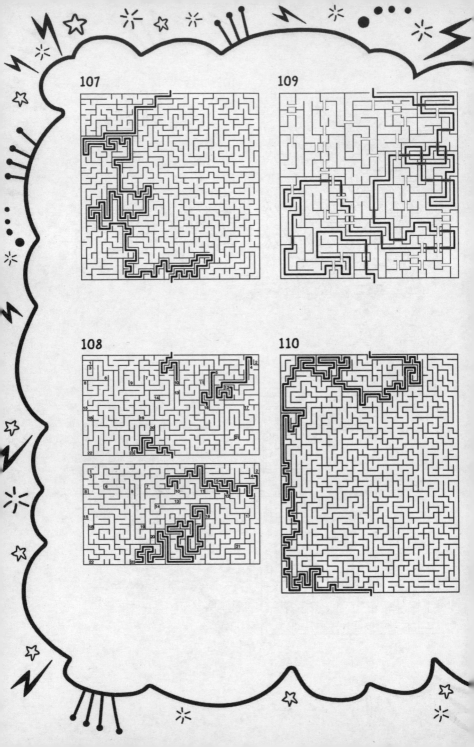

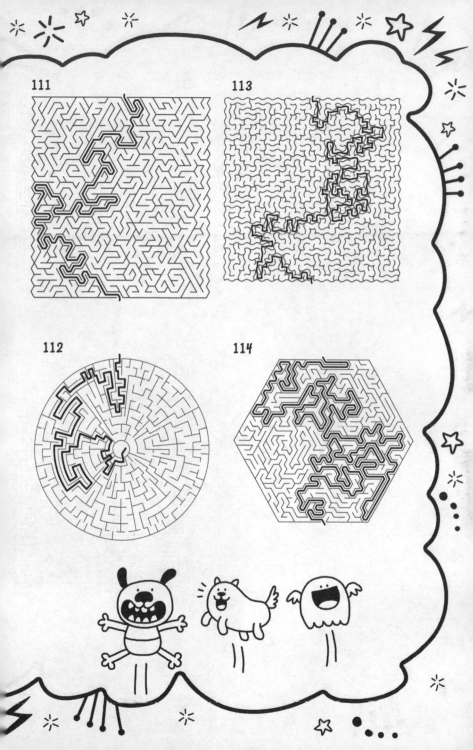

111

113

112

114

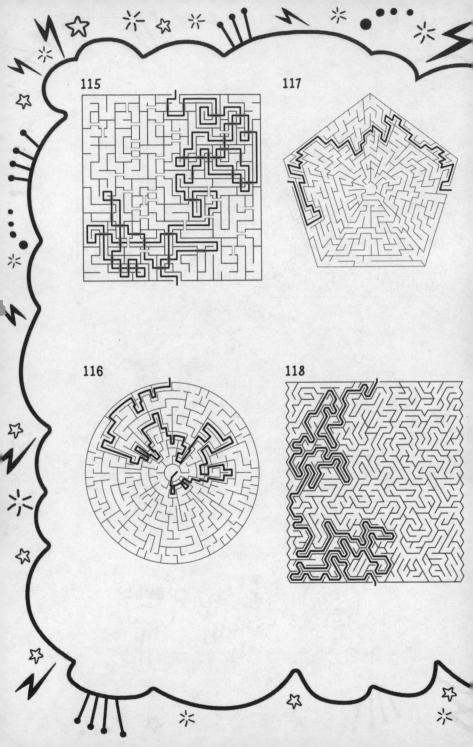

115

117

116

118

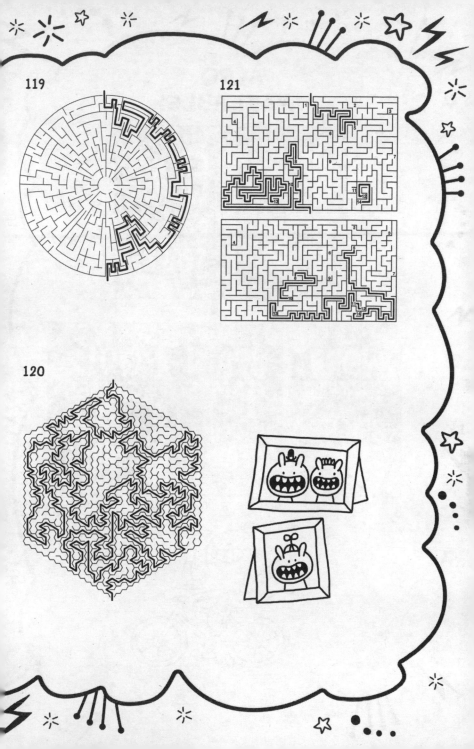

ALSO AVAILABLE:

MATHS GAMES ??? FOR ?? **BRIGHT SPARKS**
ISBN: 978-1-78055-651-2

CROSS WORDS ??? FOR ??? **BRIGHT SPARKS**
ISBN: 978-1-78055-629-1

WORD SEARCHES ??? FOR ??? **BRIGHT SPARKS**
ISBN: 978-1-78055-630-7

BRAIN GAMES ? ? FOR ? ? **BRIGHT SPARKS**
ISBN: 978-1-78055-616-1

QUIZ GAMES ??? FOR ??? **BRIGHT SPARKS**
ISBN: 978-1-78055-617-8